TEACHER'S PET PUBLICATIONS

PUZZLE PACK
for
Anne Frank: The Diary of a Young Girl
based on the diary by
Anne Frank

Written by
William T. Collins

© 2005 Teacher's Pet Publications
All Rights Reserved

The materials in this packet are copyrighted
by Teacher's Pet Publications, Inc.

These pages may be duplicated by the purchaser
for use in the purchaser's own classroom.

Copying any of these materials and distributing them
for any other purpose is a violation of the copyright laws.

© 2005 Teacher's Pet Publications, Inc.
www.tpet.com

INTRODUCTION
If you already own the LitPlan for this title, this Puzzle Pack will refresh your Unit Resource Materials and Vocabulary Resource Materials sections plus give you additional materials you can substitute into the tests. If you do not already have a complete LitPlan, these pages will give you some supplemental materials to use with your own plan. There are two main groups of materials: one set for unit words (such as characters' names, symbols, places, etc.) and one set for vocabulary words associated with the book.

WORD LIST
There is a word list for both the unit words and the vocabulary words. These lists show you which words are being used in the materials and the clues or definitions being used for those words. You may want to give students a word list with clues/definitions to help them, or you may want students to only have a word list (without clues/definitions) if you want them to work a little harder. Both are available for duplication. The word lists can also be your "calling key" for the bingo games.

FILL IN THE BLANK AND MATCHING
There are 4 each of the fill in the blank and matching worksheets for both the unit and vocabulary words. These pages can be used either as extra worksheets for students or as objective parts of a unit test. They can be done individually if students need extra help or as a whole class activity to review the material covered.

MAGIC SQUARES
The magic squares not only reinforce the material covered but also work on reasoning and math skills. Many teachers have told us that their students really enjoy doing these!

WORD SEARCH PUZZLES
The word search words go in all directions, as indicated on your answer keys. Two of the word search puzzles have the clues listed rather than the words. This makes the puzzle a little more difficult, but it reinforces the material better. Two word search puzzles have words only for students who find the clue puzzles too difficult.

CROSSWORD PUZZLES
Both unit and vocabulary word sections have 4 crossword puzzles.

BINGO CARDS
There are 32 individual bingo cards for the unit words and 32 individual bingo cards for the vocabulary words. You can use your word list as a "call list," calling the words at random and marking them off of your list as you go, or you could use the flash cards by cutting them apart and drawing the words at random from a hat (or box or whatever). To make a better review, you might ask for the definition and spelling of each word as you call it out–or you could call out the definitions and have students tell you the words they need to look for on the puzzle.

JUGGLE LETTERS
The vocabulary juggle letter game is intended to help students learn the spellings of the words. One sheet has the definitions listed on it as an extra help for students who need it or to reinforce the definitions if you choose to do so.

FLASH CARDS
We've included a set of vocabulary flash cards you can duplicate, cut, and fold for your students. Some teachers make a few sets for general use by the class; others make a set for each student. Some teachers duplicate them for each student and have the students cut & fold their own. You can cut out just the words and put them in a hat, have each student pick out one word and write the definition and a sentence for that word. Students then swap words and papers, with the next student adding a sentence of his own under the last one. You can have students swap as many times as you like. Each time the student will read the sentences written prior to his own and then add a sentence. You can cut out the words and definitions separately and play "I Have; Who Has?" Each student in the room draws a word and definition. The first student says, "I have (the name of the word). Who has the definition?" The student with the definition reads it then says, "I have (the name of the vocabulary word she has). Who has the definition?" The round continues until all words and definitions have been given.

Anne Frank Word List

No.	Word	Clue/Definition
1.	AFRICA	Continent allied forces invaded in 1942
2.	AMSTERDAM	City where the Secret Annexe was located
3.	ANNEXE	Secret ____
4.	BIRTHDAY	Day Anne's diary starts
5.	BURGLARS	They took cashboxes, sugar coupons & more
6.	CAKE	Edible Christmas present with 'Peace 1944' written on it
7.	CAMPS	Concentration ____
8.	CLOTHES	Anne's & Margo's were shabby & too small
9.	CUPBOARD	Secret entrance to the annexe
10.	DENTIST	Dussel's occupation
11.	DIARY	Anne's personal notebook
12.	DIPHTHERIA	Sickness in Eli's home that kept her away for 6 weeks
13.	DUSSEL	Elderly dentist who shares Anne's room
14.	ELLIE	She & Meip help keep spirits up in the annexe
15.	FRANK	Anne's last name
16.	FRANKFORT	City of Anne's birth
17.	GERMANY	Country of Anne's birth
18.	GESTAPO	German secret police who came for the Jews
19.	GHANDI	Freedom-loving, pacifist revolutionary in India
20.	HENK	Meip's husband
21.	HITLER	Leader of Nazi Germany
22.	HOLLAND	Country to which the Franks moved in 1933
23.	ITALY	It 'capitulated' in September 1943
24.	JEWS	Hitler wanted to exterminate all of them
25.	KISS	Peter & Anne have a 'goodnight' ____
26.	KITTY	Anne's fictitious diary friend
27.	KOLEN	____ and Co.; firm in which Mr. Frank was a partner
28.	KOOPHUIS	He was especially helpful in arranging logistics & getting food
29.	KRALER	Assumed Mr. Frank's business responsibilities
30.	LETTERS	Anne wrote them to Margot and her father
31.	LIES	Anne saw her pleading, 'Help, oh, help me . . .'
32.	LOVE	Feeling Anne has for Peter
33.	MARGOT	Anne's sister
34.	MEIP	Henk's wife; office worker; brought news & presents
35.	MOUSCHI	Peter's cat
36.	MUMMY	Mrs. Frank
37.	MYTHOLOGY	Study of Greek & Roman gods
38.	OTTO	Mr. Frank
39.	PAPER	It is more patient than man
40.	PEOPLE	'if ... there weren't any other ____ living in the world.'
41.	POTATOES	Staple vegetable at the annexe
42.	QUARREL	Verbal fight
43.	QUIET	Making no sounds

Copyrighted

Anne Frank Word List Continued

No.	Word	Clue/Definition
44.	RADIO	Clandestine 'source of courage'
45.	RAID	Air _____; bombing
46.	RAUTER	German 'big shot' in Holland; Anne mentions his speech
47.	SAUSAGE	Mr. VanDaan made meat into this
48.	SECRET	_____ Annexe
49.	SHORTHAND	Stenographer's written language
50.	STAR	Yellow ornament Jews had to wear
51.	STILL	Making no movements
52.	STUDY	Anne loved to read & _____ to pass the time
53.	TRAINS	Public transportation from which Jews were banned
54.	UPSTAIRS	Place where Anne & Peter meet in the evenings
55.	VANDAANS	Family that lived with the Franks in the annexe
56.	WESTERBORK	Work camp where many of the Franks' friend were sent

Anne Frank Fill In The Blank 1

_____ 1. German 'big shot' in Holland; Anne mentions his speech
_____ 2. Henk's wife; office worker; brought news & presents
_____ 3. Work camp where many of the Franks' friend were sent
_____ 4. She & Meip help keep spirits up in the annexe
_____ 5. City of Anne's birth
_____ 6. Leader of Nazi Germany
_____ 7. 'if ... there weren't any other ___ living in the world.'
_____ 8. German secret police who came for the Jews
_____ 9. Verbal fight
_____ 10. He was especially helpful in arranging logistics & getting food
_____ 11. Anne's personal notebook
_____ 12. Staple vegetable at the annexe
_____ 13. Day Anne's diary starts
_____ 14. Peter & Anne have a 'goodnight' ____
_____ 15. City where the Secret Annexe was located
_____ 16. Continent allied forces invaded in 1942
_____ 17. Sickness in Eli's home that kept her away for 6 weeks
_____ 18. Yellow ornament Jews had to wear
_____ 19. Anne's last name
_____ 20. ____ Annexe

Anne Frank Fill In The Blank 1 Answer Key

RAUTER	1. German 'big shot' in Holland; Anne mentions his speech
MEIP	2. Henk's wife; office worker; brought news & presents
WESTERBORK	3. Work camp where many of the Franks' friend were sent
ELLIE	4. She & Meip help keep spirits up in the annexe
FRANKFORT	5. City of Anne's birth
HITLER	6. Leader of Nazi Germany
PEOPLE	7. 'if ... there weren't any other ___ living in the world.'
GESTAPO	8. German secret police who came for the Jews
QUARREL	9. Verbal fight
KOOPHUIS	10. He was especially helpful in arranging logistics & getting food
DIARY	11. Anne's personal notebook
POTATOES	12. Staple vegetable at the annexe
BIRTHDAY	13. Day Anne's diary starts
KISS	14. Peter & Anne have a 'goodnight' ____
AMSTERDAM	15. City where the Secret Annexe was located
AFRICA	16. Continent allied forces invaded in 1942
DIPHTHERIA	17. Sickness in Eli's home that kept her away for 6 weeks
STAR	18. Yellow ornament Jews had to wear
FRANK	19. Anne's last name
SECRET	20. ____ Annexe

Anne Frank Fill In The Blank 2

_____ 1. Staple vegetable at the annexe

_____ 2. Yellow ornament Jews had to wear

_____ 3. Freedom-loving, pacifist revolutionary in India

_____ 4. Dussel's occupation

_____ 5. Sickness in Eli's home that kept her away for 6 weeks

_____ 6. Elderly dentist who shares Anne's room

_____ 7. Mr. VanDaan made meat into this

_____ 8. Place where Anne & Peter meet in the evenings

_____ 9. Leader of Nazi Germany

_____ 10. Hitler wanted to exterminate all of them

_____ 11. Anne saw her pleading, 'Help, oh, help me . . .'

_____ 12. Mr. Frank

_____ 13. Family that lived with the Franks in the annexe

_____ 14. Continent allied forces invaded in 1942

_____ 15. Anne's sister

_____ 16. He was especially helpful in arranging logistics & getting food

_____ 17. It 'capitulated' in September 1943

_____ 18. Peter's cat

_____ 19. Country of Anne's birth

_____ 20. Day Anne's diary starts

Anne Frank Fill In The Blank 2 Answer Key

POTATOES	1. Staple vegetable at the annexe
STAR	2. Yellow ornament Jews had to wear
GHANDI	3. Freedom-loving, pacifist revolutionary in India
DENTIST	4. Dussel's occupation
DIPHTHERIA	5. Sickness in Eli's home that kept her away for 6 weeks
DUSSEL	6. Elderly dentist who shares Anne's room
SAUSAGE	7. Mr. VanDaan made meat into this
UPSTAIRS	8. Place where Anne & Peter meet in the evenings
HITLER	9. Leader of Nazi Germany
JEWS	10. Hitler wanted to exterminate all of them
LIES	11. Anne saw her pleading, 'Help, oh, help me . . .'
OTTO	12. Mr. Frank
VANDAANS	13. Family that lived with the Franks in the annexe
AFRICA	14. Continent allied forces invaded in 1942
MARGOT	15. Anne's sister
KOOPHUIS	16. He was especially helpful in arranging logistics & getting food
ITALY	17. It 'capitulated' in September 1943
MOUSCHI	18. Peter's cat
GERMANY	19. Country of Anne's birth
BIRTHDAY	20. Day Anne's diary starts

Anne Frank Fill In The Blank 3

_____ 1. City of Anne's birth

_____ 2. It is more patient than man

_____ 3. Henk's wife; office worker; brought news & presents

_____ 4. Family that lived with the Franks in the annexe

_____ 5. Concentration _____

_____ 6. Anne's personal notebook

_____ 7. Elderly dentist who shares Anne's room

_____ 8. 'if ... there weren't any other ___ living in the world.'

_____ 9. Clandestine 'source of courage'

_____ 10. Edible Christmas present with 'Peace 1944' written on it

_____ 11. Country to which the Franks moved in 1933

_____ 12. Anne's & Margo's were shabby & too small

_____ 13. Meip's husband

_____ 14. Making no sounds

_____ 15. Mr. VanDaan made meat into this

_____ 16. Country of Anne's birth

_____ 17. Leader of Nazi Germany

_____ 18. Dussel's occupation

_____ 19. Anne's last name

_____ 20. Anne's fictitious diary friend

Anne Frank Fill In The Blank 3 Answer Key

FRANKFORT	1. City of Anne's birth
PAPER	2. It is more patient than man
MEIP	3. Henk's wife; office worker; brought news & presents
VANDAANS	4. Family that lived with the Franks in the annexe
CAMPS	5. Concentration _____
DIARY	6. Anne's personal notebook
DUSSEL	7. Elderly dentist who shares Anne's room
PEOPLE	8. 'if ... there weren't any other ___ living in the world.'
RADIO	9. Clandestine 'source of courage'
CAKE	10. Edible Christmas present with 'Peace 1944' written on it
HOLLAND	11. Country to which the Franks moved in 1933
CLOTHES	12. Anne's & Margo's were shabby & too small
HENK	13. Meip's husband
QUIET	14. Making no sounds
SAUSAGE	15. Mr. VanDaan made meat into this
GERMANY	16. Country of Anne's birth
HITLER	17. Leader of Nazi Germany
DENTIST	18. Dussel's occupation
FRANK	19. Anne's last name
KITTY	20. Anne's fictitious diary friend

Anne Frank Fill In The Blank 4

_____   1. Mr. VanDaan made meat into this
_____   2. Public transportation from which Jews were banned
_____   3. Dussel's occupation
_____   4. Place where Anne & Peter meet in the evenings
_____   5. City of Anne's birth
_____   6. Day Anne's diary starts
_____   7. Anne's & Margo's were shabby & too small
_____   8. Anne saw her pleading, 'Help, oh, help me . . .'
_____   9. Anne's personal notebook
_____ 10. Making no sounds
_____ 11. Peter's cat
_____ 12. Making no movements
_____ 13. Assumed Mr. Frank's business responsibilities
_____ 14. 'if ... there weren't any other ___ living in the world.'
_____ 15. Anne wrote them to Margot and her father
_____ 16. Elderly dentist who shares Anne's room
_____ 17. Leader of Nazi Germany
_____ 18. Henk's wife; office worker; brought news & presents
_____ 19. Work camp where many of the Franks' friend were sent
_____ 20. Secret entrance to the annexe

Anne Frank Fill In The Blank 4 Answer Key

SAUSAGE	1. Mr. VanDaan made meat into this
TRAINS	2. Public transportation from which Jews were banned
DENTIST	3. Dussel's occupation
UPSTAIRS	4. Place where Anne & Peter meet in the evenings
FRANKFORT	5. City of Anne's birth
BIRTHDAY	6. Day Anne's diary starts
CLOTHES	7. Anne's & Margo's were shabby & too small
LIES	8. Anne saw her pleading, 'Help, oh, help me . . .'
DIARY	9. Anne's personal notebook
QUIET	10. Making no sounds
MOUSCHI	11. Peter's cat
STILL	12. Making no movements
KRALER	13. Assumed Mr. Frank's business responsibilities
PEOPLE	14. 'if ... there weren't any other ___ living in the world.'
LETTERS	15. Anne wrote them to Margot and her father
DUSSEL	16. Elderly dentist who shares Anne's room
HITLER	17. Leader of Nazi Germany
MEIP	18. Henk's wife; office worker; brought news & presents
WESTERBORK	19. Work camp where many of the Franks' friend were sent
CUPBOARD	20. Secret entrance to the annexe

Anne Frank Matching 1

___ 1. UPSTAIRS   A. Sickness in Eli's home that kept her away for 6 weeks
___ 2. DIPHTHERIA   B. Edible Christmas present with 'Peace 1944' written on it
___ 3. MUMMY   C. Mrs. Frank
___ 4. RADIO   D. Peter's cat
___ 5. MOUSCHI   E. Anne's sister
___ 6. QUIET   F. ___ and Co.; firm in which Mr. Frank was a partner
___ 7. MEIP   G. Anne loved to read & _____ to pass the time
___ 8. ITALY   H. She & Meip help keep spirits up in the annexe
___ 9. MARGOT   I. Anne wrote them to Margot and her father
___10. STAR   J. German 'big shot' in Holland; Anne mentions his speech
___11. DUSSEL   K. Stenographer's written language
___12. RAUTER   L. Country of Anne's birth
___13. GERMANY   M. Clandestine 'source of courage'
___14. OTTO   N. Making no sounds
___15. KOLEN   O. Peter & Anne have a 'goodnight' ____
___16. CAKE   P. It is more patient than man
___17. KISS   Q. Air _____; bombing
___18. SHORTHAND   R. Henk's wife; office worker; brought news & presents
___19. POTATOES   S. Staple vegetable at the annexe
___20. STUDY   T. Place where Anne & Peter meet in the evenings
___21. JEWS   U. Elderly dentist who shares Anne's room
___22. LETTERS   V. Yellow ornament Jews had to wear
___23. PAPER   W. Hitler wanted to exterminate all of them
___24. ELLIE   X. Mr. Frank
___25. RAID   Y. It 'capitulated' in September 1943

Anne Frank Matching 1 Answer Key

T - 1. UPSTAIRS	A. Sickness in Eli's home that kept her away for 6 weeks
A - 2. DIPHTHERIA	B. Edible Christmas present with 'Peace 1944' written on it
C - 3. MUMMY	C. Mrs. Frank
M - 4. RADIO	D. Peter's cat
D - 5. MOUSCHI	E. Anne's sister
N - 6. QUIET	F. ___ and Co.; firm in which Mr. Frank was a partner
R - 7. MEIP	G. Anne loved to read & _____ to pass the time
Y - 8. ITALY	H. She & Meip help keep spirits up in the annexe
E - 9. MARGOT	I. Anne wrote them to Margot and her father
V - 10. STAR	J. German 'big shot' in Holland; Anne mentions his speech
U - 11. DUSSEL	K. Stenographer's written language
J - 12. RAUTER	L. Country of Anne's birth
L - 13. GERMANY	M. Clandestine 'source of courage'
X - 14. OTTO	N. Making no sounds
F - 15. KOLEN	O. Peter & Anne have a 'goodnight' ____
B - 16. CAKE	P. It is more patient than man
O - 17. KISS	Q. Air _____; bombing
K - 18. SHORTHAND	R. Henk's wife; office worker; brought news & presents
S - 19. POTATOES	S. Staple vegetable at the annexe
G - 20. STUDY	T. Place where Anne & Peter meet in the evenings
W - 21. JEWS	U. Elderly dentist who shares Anne's room
I - 22. LETTERS	V. Yellow ornament Jews had to wear
P - 23. PAPER	W. Hitler wanted to exterminate all of them
H - 24. ELLIE	X. Mr. Frank
Q - 25. RAID	Y. It 'capitulated' in September 1943

Anne Frank Matching 2

___ 1. DIPHTHERIA   A. It 'capitulated' in September 1943
___ 2. AMSTERDAM   B. Staple vegetable at the annexe
___ 3. CUPBOARD   C. Country to which the Franks moved in 1933
___ 4. BIRTHDAY   D. ____ Annexe
___ 5. STUDY   E. German secret police who came for the Jews
___ 6. DIARY   F. Anne wrote them to Margot and her father
___ 7. KRALER   G. Assumed Mr. Frank's business responsibilities
___ 8. KISS   H. Concentration _____
___ 9. FRANK   I. Mr. VanDaan made meat into this
___10. LETTERS   J. Continent allied forces invaded in 1942
___11. STILL   K. Making no movements
___12. CLOTHES   L. Family that lived with the Franks in the annexe
___13. AFRICA   M. Anne loved to read & _____ to pass the time
___14. VANDAANS   N. Anne's last name
___15. ITALY   O. City where the Secret Annexe was located
___16. GESTAPO   P. Anne's personal notebook
___17. SAUSAGE   Q. Mrs. Frank
___18. ELLIE   R. Secret entrance to the annexe
___19. POTATOES   S. ___ and Co.; firm in which Mr. Frank was a partner
___20. MUMMY   T. Sickness in Eli's home that kept her away for 6 weeks
___21. RAID   U. Air _____; bombing
___22. CAMPS   V. Anne's & Margo's were shabby & too small
___23. HOLLAND   W. Day Anne's diary starts
___24. KOLEN   X. Peter & Anne have a 'goodnight' ____
___25. SECRET   Y. She & Meip help keep spirits up in the annexe

Anne Frank Matching 2 Answer Key

T - 1. DIPHTHERIA	A. It 'capitulated' in September 1943
O - 2. AMSTERDAM	B. Staple vegetable at the annexe
R - 3. CUPBOARD	C. Country to which the Franks moved in 1933
W - 4. BIRTHDAY	D. ____ Annexe
M - 5. STUDY	E. German secret police who came for the Jews
P - 6. DIARY	F. Anne wrote them to Margot and her father
G - 7. KRALER	G. Assumed Mr. Frank's business responsibilities
X - 8. KISS	H. Concentration _____
N - 9. FRANK	I. Mr. VanDaan made meat into this
F - 10. LETTERS	J. Continent allied forces invaded in 1942
K - 11. STILL	K. Making no movements
V - 12. CLOTHES	L. Family that lived with the Franks in the annexe
J - 13. AFRICA	M. Anne loved to read & ____ to pass the time
L - 14. VANDAANS	N. Anne's last name
A - 15. ITALY	O. City where the Secret Annexe was located
E - 16. GESTAPO	P. Anne's personal notebook
I - 17. SAUSAGE	Q. Mrs. Frank
Y - 18. ELLIE	R. Secret entrance to the annexe
B - 19. POTATOES	S. ___ and Co.; firm in which Mr. Frank was a partner
Q - 20. MUMMY	T. Sickness in Eli's home that kept her away for 6 weeks
U - 21. RAID	U. Air _____; bombing
H - 22. CAMPS	V. Anne's & Margo's were shabby & too small
C - 23. HOLLAND	W. Day Anne's diary starts
S - 24. KOLEN	X. Peter & Anne have a 'goodnight' ____
D - 25. SECRET	Y. She & Meip help keep spirits up in the annexe

Anne Frank Matching 3

___ 1. FRANK   A. Air _____; bombing
___ 2. KRALER   B. Secret ____
___ 3. ELLIE   C. Yellow ornament Jews had to wear
___ 4. WESTERBORK   D. Hitler wanted to exterminate all of them
___ 5. LOVE   E. Dussel's occupation
___ 6. ANNEXE   F. 'if ... there weren't any other ___ living in the world.'
___ 7. RAID   G. Place where Anne & Peter meet in the evenings
___ 8. STILL   H. Mr. VanDaan made meat into this
___ 9. DENTIST   I. Meip's husband
___10. HENK   J. ___ and Co.; firm in which Mr. Frank was a partner
___11. RADIO   K. Anne saw her pleading, 'Help, oh, help me . . .'
___12. KITTY   L. German secret police who came for the Jews
___13. KOOPHUIS   M. She & Meip help keep spirits up in the annexe
___14. RAUTER   N. Concentration _____
___15. QUARREL   O. Verbal fight
___16. GESTAPO   P. Work camp where many of the Franks' friend were sent
___17. KOLEN   Q. Feeling Anne has for Peter
___18. UPSTAIRS   R. Anne's last name
___19. SAUSAGE   S. Anne's fictitious diary friend
___20. LIES   T. Making no movements
___21. STAR   U. He was especially helpful in arranging logistics & getting food
___22. FRANKFORT   V. City of Anne's birth
___23. JEWS   W. Assumed Mr. Frank's business responsibilities
___24. CAMPS   X. German 'big shot' in Holland; Anne mentions his speech
___25. PEOPLE   Y. Clandestine 'source of courage'

Anne Frank Matching 3 Answer Key

R - 1. FRANK   A. Air _____; bombing
W - 2. KRALER   B. Secret ____
M - 3. ELLIE   C. Yellow ornament Jews had to wear
P - 4. WESTERBORK   D. Hitler wanted to exterminate all of them
Q - 5. LOVE   E. Dussel's occupation
B - 6. ANNEXE   F. 'if ... there weren't any other ___ living in the world.'
A - 7. RAID   G. Place where Anne & Peter meet in the evenings
T - 8. STILL   H. Mr. VanDaan made meat into this
E - 9. DENTIST   I. Meip's husband
I - 10. HENK   J. ___ and Co.; firm in which Mr. Frank was a partner
Y - 11. RADIO   K. Anne saw her pleading, 'Help, oh, help me . . .'
S - 12. KITTY   L. German secret police who came for the Jews
U - 13. KOOPHUIS   M. She & Meip help keep spirits up in the annexe
X - 14. RAUTER   N. Concentration _____
O - 15. QUARREL   O. Verbal fight
L - 16. GESTAPO   P. Work camp where many of the Franks' friend were sent
J - 17. KOLEN   Q. Feeling Anne has for Peter
G - 18. UPSTAIRS   R. Anne's last name
H - 19. SAUSAGE   S. Anne's fictitious diary friend
K - 20. LIES   T. Making no movements
C - 21. STAR   U. He was especially helpful in arranging logistics & getting food
V - 22. FRANKFORT   V. City of Anne's birth
D - 23. JEWS   W. Assumed Mr. Frank's business responsibilities
N - 24. CAMPS   X. German 'big shot' in Holland; Anne mentions his speech
F - 25. PEOPLE   Y. Clandestine 'source of courage'

Anne Frank Matching 4

___ 1. GESTAPO A. German 'big shot' in Holland; Anne mentions his speech
___ 2. ELLIE B. Day Anne's diary starts
___ 3. ITALY C. Henk's wife; office worker; brought news & presents
___ 4. MUMMY D. Anne loved to read & _____ to pass the time
___ 5. MEIP E. Assumed Mr. Frank's business responsibilities
___ 6. SECRET F. Dussel's occupation
___ 7. SAUSAGE G. It 'capitulated' in September 1943
___ 8. BURGLARS H. City where the Secret Annexe was located
___ 9. RAUTER I. Anne's fictitious diary friend
___10. GHANDI J. Staple vegetable at the annexe
___11. AFRICA K. Mr. VanDaan made meat into this
___12. DENTIST L. 'if ... there weren't any other ___ living in the world.'
___13. POTATOES M. Edible Christmas present with 'Peace 1944' written on it
___14. HENK N. Meip's husband
___15. LETTERS O. Freedom-loving, pacifist revolutionary in India
___16. JEWS P. She & Meip help keep spirits up in the annexe
___17. KRALER Q. Stenographer's written language
___18. PEOPLE R. Secret entrance to the annexe
___19. CUPBOARD S. German secret police who came for the Jews
___20. CAKE T. ____ Annexe
___21. AMSTERDAM U. Continent allied forces invaded in 1942
___22. SHORTHAND V. Hitler wanted to exterminate all of them
___23. BIRTHDAY W. They took cashboxes, sugar coupons & more
___24. STUDY X. Mrs. Frank
___25. KITTY Y. Anne wrote them to Margot and her father

Anne Frank Matching 4 Answer Key

S - 1.	GESTAPO	A.	German 'big shot' in Holland; Anne mentions his speech
P - 2.	ELLIE	B.	Day Anne's diary starts
G - 3.	ITALY	C.	Henk's wife; office worker; brought news & presents
X - 4.	MUMMY	D.	Anne loved to read & _____ to pass the time
C - 5.	MEIP	E.	Assumed Mr. Frank's business responsibilities
T - 6.	SECRET	F.	Dussel's occupation
K - 7.	SAUSAGE	G.	It 'capitulated' in September 1943
W - 8.	BURGLARS	H.	City where the Secret Annexe was located
A - 9.	RAUTER	I.	Anne's fictitious diary friend
O - 10.	GHANDI	J.	Staple vegetable at the annexe
U - 11.	AFRICA	K.	Mr. VanDaan made meat into this
F - 12.	DENTIST	L.	'if ... there weren't any other ___ living in the world.'
J - 13.	POTATOES	M.	Edible Christmas present with 'Peace 1944' written on it
N - 14.	HENK	N.	Meip's husband
Y - 15.	LETTERS	O.	Freedom-loving, pacifist revolutionary in India
V - 16.	JEWS	P.	She & Meip help keep spirits up in the annexe
E - 17.	KRALER	Q.	Stenographer's written language
L - 18.	PEOPLE	R.	Secret entrance to the annexe
R - 19.	CUPBOARD	S.	German secret police who came for the Jews
M - 20.	CAKE	T.	_____ Annexe
H - 21.	AMSTERDAM	U.	Continent allied forces invaded in 1942
Q - 22.	SHORTHAND	V.	Hitler wanted to exterminate all of them
B - 23.	BIRTHDAY	W.	They took cashboxes, sugar coupons & more
D - 24.	STUDY	X.	Mrs. Frank
I - 25.	KITTY	Y.	Anne wrote them to Margot and her father

Anne Frank Magic Squares 1

Match the definition with the vocabulary word. Put your answers in the magic squares below. When your answers are correct, all columns and rows will add to the same number.

A. DIARY
B. LETTERS
C. MOUSCHI
D. HITLER
E. RAID
F. FRANKFORT
G. ITALY
H. RADIO
I. MYTHOLOGY
J. UPSTAIRS
K. GESTAPO
L. KISS
M. STUDY
N. CUPBOARD
O. QUIET
P. DENTIST

1. Secret entrance to the annexe
2. It 'capitulated' in September 1943
3. Peter & Anne have a 'goodnight' ____
4. Anne's personal notebook
5. German secret police who came for the Jews
6. Anne wrote them to Margot and her father
7. Anne loved to read & ____ to pass the time
8. Clandestine 'source of courage'
9. Air ____; bombing
10. Dussel's occupation
11. Peter's cat
12. Place where Anne & Peter meet in the evenings
13. Leader of Nazi Germany
14. Study of Greek & Roman gods
15. City of Anne's birth
16. Making no sounds

A=	B=	C=	D=
E=	F=	G=	H=
I=	J=	K=	L=
M=	N=	O=	P=

Anne Frank Magic Squares 1 Answer Key

Match the definition with the vocabulary word. Put your answers in the magic squares below. When your answers are correct, all columns and rows will add to the same number.

A. DIARY
B. LETTERS
C. MOUSCHI
D. HITLER
E. RAID
F. FRANKFORT
G. ITALY
H. RADIO
I. MYTHOLOGY
J. UPSTAIRS
K. GESTAPO
L. KISS
M. STUDY
N. CUPBOARD
O. QUIET
P. DENTIST

1. Secret entrance to the annexe
2. It 'capitulated' in September 1943
3. Peter & Anne have a 'goodnight' ____
4. Anne's personal notebook
5. German secret police who came for the Jews
6. Anne wrote them to Margot and her father
7. Anne loved to read & ____ to pass the time
8. Clandestine 'source of courage'
9. Air ____; bombing
10. Dussel's occupation
11. Peter's cat
12. Place where Anne & Peter meet in the evenings
13. Leader of Nazi Germany
14. Study of Greek & Roman gods
15. City of Anne's birth
16. Making no sounds

A=4	B=6	C=11	D=13
E=9	F=15	G=2	H=8
I=14	J=12	K=5	L=3
M=7	N=1	O=16	P=10

Anne Frank Magic Squares 2

Match the definition with the vocabulary word. Put your answers in the magic squares below. When your answers are correct, all columns and rows will add to the same number.

A. OTTO
B. DENTIST
C. DIPHTHERIA
D. FRANK
E. TRAINS
F. RAID
G. KITTY
H. DIARY
I. SECRET
J. LOVE
K. VANDAANS
L. RAUTER
M. GHANDI
N. PEOPLE
O. BIRTHDAY
P. LIES

1. Anne's personal notebook
2. Mr. Frank
3. Dussel's occupation
4. Anne's fictitious diary friend
5. Feeling Anne has for Peter
6. Day Anne's diary starts
7. Anne saw her pleading, 'Help, oh, help me . . .'
8. ____ Annexe
9. Family that lived with the Franks in the annexe
10. 'if ... there weren't any other ___ living in the world.'
11. Freedom-loving, pacifist revolutionary in India
12. German 'big shot' in Holland; Anne mentions his speech
13. Public transportation from which Jews were banned
14. Anne's last name
15. Sickness in Eli's home that kept her away for 6 weeks
16. Air _____; bombing

A=	B=	C=	D=
E=	F=	G=	H=
I=	J=	K=	L=
M=	N=	O=	P=

Anne Frank Magic Squares 2 Answer Key

Match the definition with the vocabulary word. Put your answers in the magic squares below. When your answers are correct, all columns and rows will add to the same number.

A. OTTO
B. DENTIST
C. DIPHTHERIA
D. FRANK
E. TRAINS
F. RAID
G. KITTY
H. DIARY
I. SECRET
J. LOVE
K. VANDAANS
L. RAUTER
M. GHANDI
N. PEOPLE
O. BIRTHDAY
P. LIES

1. Anne's personal notebook
2. Mr. Frank
3. Dussel's occupation
4. Anne's fictitious diary friend
5. Feeling Anne has for Peter
6. Day Anne's diary starts
7. Anne saw her pleading, 'Help, oh, help me . . .'
8. ____ Annexe
9. Family that lived with the Franks in the annexe
10. 'if ... there weren't any other ___ living in the world.'
11. Freedom-loving, pacifist revolutionary in India
12. German 'big shot' in Holland; Anne mentions his speech
13. Public transportation from which Jews were banned
14. Anne's last name
15. Sickness in Eli's home that kept her away for 6 weeks
16. Air _____; bombing

A=2	B=3	C=15	D=14
E=13	F=16	G=4	H=1
I=8	J=5	K=9	L=12
M=11	N=10	O=6	P=7

Anne Frank Magic Squares 3

Match the definition with the vocabulary word. Put your answers in the magic squares below. When your answers are correct, all columns and rows will add to the same number.

A. CAKE   E. RAID   I. OTTO   M. KOOPHUIS
B. GHANDI   F. HITLER   J. GESTAPO   N. KOLEN
C. PEOPLE   G. WESTERBORK   K. AMSTERDAM   O. QUIET
D. DIPHTHERIA   H. SECRET   L. KRALER   P. VANDAANS

1. Making no sounds
2. Sickness in Eli's home that kept her away for 6 weeks
3. German secret police who came for the Jews
4. Air _____; bombing
5. Mr. Frank
6. Leader of Nazi Germany
7. Family that lived with the Franks in the annexe
8. 'if ... there weren't any other ___ living in the world.'
9. ____ Annexe
10. City where the Secret Annexe was located
11. Edible Christmas present with 'Peace 1944' written on it
12. ___ and Co.; firm in which Mr. Frank was a partner
13. Freedom-loving, pacifist revolutionary in India
14. He was especially helpful in arranging logistics & getting food
15. Work camp where many of the Franks' friend were sent
16. Assumed Mr. Frank's business responsibilities

A=	B=	C=	D=
E=	F=	G=	H=
I=	J=	K=	L=
M=	N=	O=	P=

Anne Frank Magic Squares 3 Answer Key

Match the definition with the vocabulary word. Put your answers in the magic squares below. When your answers are correct, all columns and rows will add to the same number.

A. CAKE
B. GHANDI
C. PEOPLE
D. DIPHTHERIA
E. RAID
F. HITLER
G. WESTERBORK
H. SECRET
I. OTTO
J. GESTAPO
K. AMSTERDAM
L. KRALER
M. KOOPHUIS
N. KOLEN
O. QUIET
P. VANDAANS

1. Making no sounds
2. Sickness in Eli's home that kept her away for 6 weeks
3. German secret police who came for the Jews
4. Air _____; bombing
5. Mr. Frank
6. Leader of Nazi Germany
7. Family that lived with the Franks in the annexe
8. 'if ... there weren't any other ___ living in the world.'
9. ____ Annexe
10. City where the Secret Annexe was located
11. Edible Christmas present with 'Peace 1944' written on it
12. ___ and Co.; firm in which Mr. Frank was a partner
13. Freedom-loving, pacifist revolutionary in India
14. He was especially helpful in arranging logistics & getting food
15. Work camp where many of the Franks' friend were sent
16. Assumed Mr. Frank's business responsibilities

A=11	B=13	C=8	D=2
E=4	F=6	G=15	H=9
I=5	J=3	K=10	L=16
M=14	N=12	O=1	P=7

Anne Frank Magic Squares 4

Match the definition with the vocabulary word. Put your answers in the magic squares below. When your answers are correct, all columns and rows will add to the same number.

A. LIES
B. MEIP
C. OTTO
D. ITALY
E. SAUSAGE
F. GHANDI
G. UPSTAIRS
H. HITLER
I. DUSSEL
J. CUPBOARD
K. LETTERS
L. MOUSCHI
M. CAKE
N. KOOPHUIS
O. ANNEXE
P. KOLEN

1. Leader of Nazi Germany
2. Edible Christmas present with 'Peace 1944' written on it
3. Henk's wife; office worker; brought news & presents
4. Anne wrote them to Margot and her father
5. Secret entrance to the annexe
6. Mr. Frank
7. ___ and Co.; firm in which Mr. Frank was a partner
8. Mr. VanDaan made meat into this
9. Secret ____
10. Freedom-loving, pacifist revolutionary in India
11. Elderly dentist who shares Anne's room
12. It 'capitulated' in September 1943
13. Anne saw her pleading, 'Help, oh, help me . . .'
14. Peter's cat
15. Place where Anne & Peter meet in the evenings
16. He was especially helpful in arranging logistics & getting food

A=	B=	C=	D=
E=	F=	G=	H=
I=	J=	K=	L=
M=	N=	O=	P=

Anne Frank Magic Squares 4 Answer Key

Match the definition with the vocabulary word. Put your answers in the magic squares below. When your answers are correct, all columns and rows will add to the same number.

A. LIES
B. MEIP
C. OTTO
D. ITALY
E. SAUSAGE
F. GHANDI
G. UPSTAIRS
H. HITLER
I. DUSSEL
J. CUPBOARD
K. LETTERS
L. MOUSCHI
M. CAKE
N. KOOPHUIS
O. ANNEXE
P. KOLEN

1. Leader of Nazi Germany
2. Edible Christmas present with 'Peace 1944' written on it
3. Henk's wife; office worker; brought news & presents
4. Anne wrote them to Margot and her father
5. Secret entrance to the annexe
6. Mr. Frank
7. ___ and Co.; firm in which Mr. Frank was a partner
8. Mr. VanDaan made meat into this
9. Secret ____
10. Freedom-loving, pacifist revolutionary in India
11. Elderly dentist who shares Anne's room
12. It 'capitulated' in September 1943
13. Anne saw her pleading, 'Help, oh, help me . . .'
14. Peter's cat
15. Place where Anne & Peter meet in the evenings
16. He was especially helpful in arranging logistics & getting food

A=13	B=3	C=6	D=12
E=8	F=10	G=15	H=1
I=11	J=5	K=4	L=14
M=2	N=16	O=9	P=7

Anne Frank Word Search 1

```
L E T T E R S Q U I E T C S M M V
G R Z V E D A C I R F A W M O D N
B K A W K L N C D Y A E C A U G R
Y M M U M O L F L T J D T R S R S
S J N R T S L I K T J H I G C E Q
V V P A N E X E E I Z H I O H P B
B L F I X F R A N K F O R T I A Z
F Q A D H A R F R N L L O S L P B
I R K W T K J A S E B L X I Z E L
T B P S T P L E N H C A D T G O R
A N N E X E C D Y K S N F N V P H
L R K N R R A X P Y T D X E W L M
Y N K I E W K F I N I P G D T E B
Y D U T S H E S E I L D I A R Y W
O T T O Q S Y V M C L E R R A U Q
```

'if ... there weren't any other ___ living in the world.' (6)
Air _____; bombing (4)
Anne loved to read & _____ to pass the time (5)
Anne saw her pleading, 'Help, oh, help me . . .' (4)
Anne wrote them to Margot and her father (7)
Anne's & Margo's were shabby & too small (7)
Anne's fictitious diary friend (5)
Anne's last name (5)
Anne's personal notebook (5)
Anne's sister (6)
Assumed Mr. Frank's business responsibilities (6)
City of Anne's birth (9)
Clandestine 'source of courage' (5)
Continent allied forces invaded in 1942 (6)
Country to which the Franks moved in 1933 (7)
Dussel's occupation (7)
Edible Christmas present with 'Peace 1944' written on it (4)
Feeling Anne has for Peter (4)
German 'big shot' in Holland; Anne mentions his speech (6)
Henk's wife; office worker; brought news & presents (4)
Hitler wanted to exterminate all of them (4)
It 'capitulated' in September 1943 (5)
It is more patient than man (5)
Leader of Nazi Germany (6)
Making no movements (5)
Making no sounds (5)
Meip's husband (4)
Mr. Frank (4)
Mrs. Frank (5)
Peter & Anne have a 'goodnight' ____ (4)
Peter's cat (7)
Public transportation from which Jews were banned (6)
Secret ____ (6)
She & Meip help keep spirits up in the annexe (5)
Verbal fight (7)
Yellow ornament Jews had to wear (4)
___ and Co.; firm in which Mr. Frank was a partner (5)
____ Annexe (6)

Anne Frank Word Search 1 Answer key

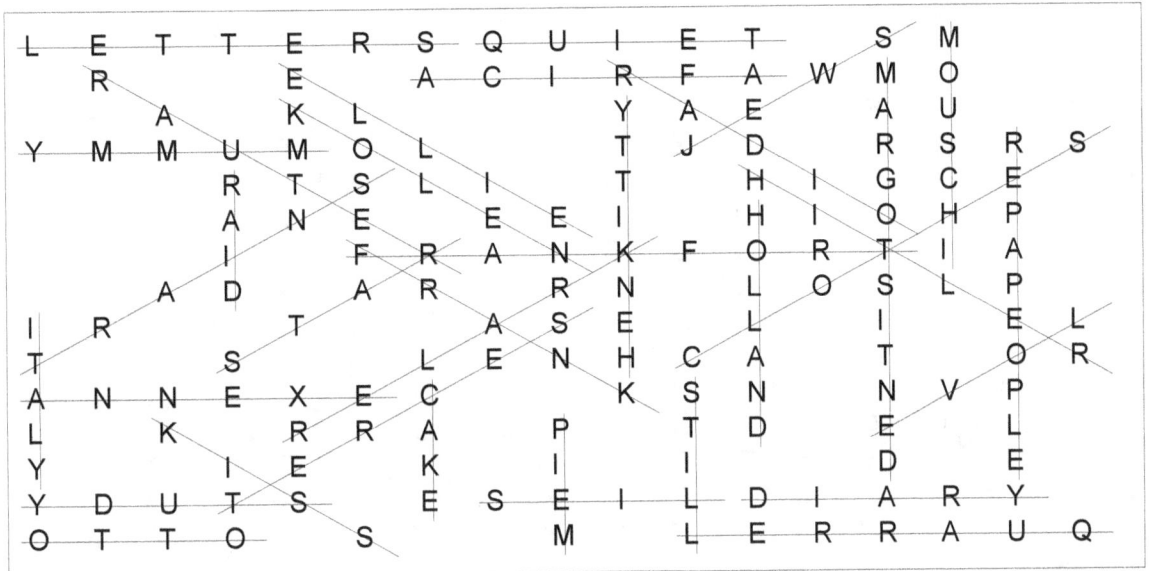

'if ... there weren't any other ___ living in the world.' (6)
Air _____; bombing (4)
Anne loved to read & _____ to pass the time (5)
Anne saw her pleading, 'Help, oh, help me . . .' (4)
Anne wrote them to Margot and her father (7)
Anne's & Margo's were shabby & too small (7)
Anne's fictitious diary friend (5)
Anne's last name (5)
Anne's personal notebook (5)
Anne's sister (6)
Assumed Mr. Frank's business responsibilities (6)
City of Anne's birth (9)
Clandestine 'source of courage' (5)
Continent allied forces invaded in 1942 (6)
Country to which the Franks moved in 1933 (7)
Dussel's occupation (7)
Edible Christmas present with 'Peace 1944' written on it (4)
Feeling Anne has for Peter (4)
German 'big shot' in Holland; Anne mentions his speech (6)
Henk's wife; office worker; brought news & presents (4)
Hitler wanted to exterminate all of them (4)
It 'capitulated' in September 1943 (5)
It is more patient than man (5)
Leader of Nazi Germany (6)
Making no movements (5)
Making no sounds (5)
Meip's husband (4)
Mr. Frank (4)
Mrs. Frank (5)
Peter & Anne have a 'goodnight' ____ (4)
Peter's cat (7)
Public transportation from which Jews were banned (6)
Secret ____ (6)
She & Meip help keep spirits up in the annexe (5)
Verbal fight (7)
Yellow ornament Jews had to wear (4)
___ and Co.; firm in which Mr. Frank was a partner (5)
____ Annexe (6)

Anne Frank Word Search 2

```
M O T T O U P S T A I R S Z Z S F
J Y S H O R T H A N D R E T U A R
M S T T R R N T J D L O C P S U A
P U A H A D X R I P J R T M S N
E B M T O U D Y N A M R E G O A K
O U S M S L D I T R I I T W U G F
P R T S Y U O S O Y U N G K S E O
L G E P T B E G Y Q L M S R C H R
E L R S A G F A Y E E O E Z H E T
K A D X P P D D R I T L V T I N S
A R A L E H E R P Z T N X E N K N
C S M I T P A R X I E L I E S L V
Q S L R H U T C H M R X L S Z D S
V L I W Q K I T T Y S O I R A I D
E B P O T A T O E S K K R A L E R
```

'if ... there weren't any other ___ living in the world.' (6)

Air _____; bombing (4)

Anne loved to read & _____ to pass the time (5)

Anne saw her pleading, 'Help, oh, help me . . .' (4)

Anne wrote them to Margot and her father (7)

Anne's fictitious diary friend (5)

Anne's personal notebook (5)

Assumed Mr. Frank's business responsibilities (6)

City of Anne's birth (9)

City where the Secret Annexe was located (9)

Clandestine 'source of courage' (5)

Country of Anne's birth (7)

Day Anne's diary starts (8)

Edible Christmas present with 'Peace 1944' written on it (4)

Elderly dentist who shares Anne's room (6)

Feeling Anne has for Peter (4)

German 'big shot' in Holland; Anne mentions his speech (6)

German secret police who came for the Jews (7)

Henk's wife; office worker; brought news & presents (4)

Hitler wanted to exterminate all of them (4)

It is more patient than man (5)

Leader of Nazi Germany (6)

Making no sounds (5)

Meip's husband (4)

Mr. Frank (4)

Mr. VanDaan made meat into this (7)

Mrs. Frank (5)

Peter & Anne have a 'goodnight' ____ (4)

Peter's cat (7)

Place where Anne & Peter meet in the evenings (8)

Public transportation from which Jews were banned (6)

She & Meip help keep spirits up in the annexe (5)

Staple vegetable at the annexe (8)

Stenographer's written language (9)

Study of Greek & Roman gods (9)

They took cashboxes, sugar coupons & more (8)

Verbal fight (7)

Yellow ornament Jews had to wear (4)

___ and Co.; firm in which Mr. Frank was a partner (5)

____ Annexe (6)

Anne Frank Word Search 2 Answer Key

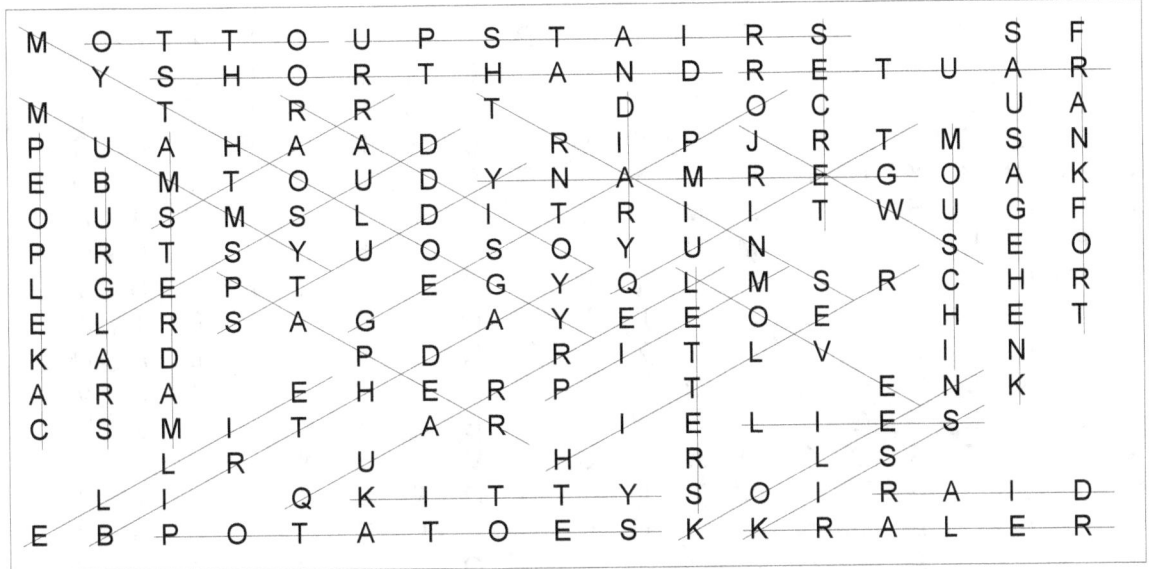

'if ... there weren't any other ___ living in the world.' (6)
Air _____; bombing (4)
Anne loved to read & _____ to pass the time (5)
Anne saw her pleading, 'Help, oh, help me . . .' (4)
Anne wrote them to Margot and her father (7)
Anne's fictitious diary friend (5)
Anne's personal notebook (5)
Assumed Mr. Frank's business responsibilities (6)
City of Anne's birth (9)
City where the Secret Annexe was located (9)
Clandestine 'source of courage' (5)
Country of Anne's birth (7)
Day Anne's diary starts (8)
Edible Christmas present with 'Peace 1944' written on it (4)
Elderly dentist who shares Anne's room (6)
Feeling Anne has for Peter (4)
German 'big shot' in Holland; Anne mentions his speech (6)
German secret police who came for the Jews (7)
Henk's wife; office worker; brought news & presents (4)
Hitler wanted to exterminate all of them (4)
It is more patient than man (5)
Leader of Nazi Germany (6)
Making no sounds (5)
Meip's husband (4)
Mr. Frank (4)
Mr. VanDaan made meat into this (7)
Mrs. Frank (5)
Peter & Anne have a 'goodnight' ____ (4)
Peter's cat (7)
Place where Anne & Peter meet in the evenings (8)
Public transportation from which Jews were banned (6)
She & Meip help keep spirits up in the annexe (5)
Staple vegetable at the annexe (8)
Stenographer's written language (9)
Study of Greek & Roman gods (9)
They took cashboxes, sugar coupons & more (8)
Verbal fight (7)
Yellow ornament Jews had to wear (4)
___ and Co.; firm in which Mr. Frank was a partner (5)
____ Annexe (6)

Anne Frank Word Search 3

```
Y C S N I A R T R T E R C E S K L A B K
M W M X T V K S Z Q U Q A R W O M U D
N V O B A K I C S P K K O K K V S G T
B C U C L R T N B N L B K N E E T R C
K I S S Y N E K O Y R O I A H Q R L D
J B C V E I R A M D E T T R O U A H
H B H D L A R M U T A H T F L A R G
T M I L L D U T S T Q Y O Y V R M T M
V P E E F M S E S E H T O L C A M J
D S R I S A W E E X E N N A I N E A D
V W R Q P R G X O J J Y M R P D L R V
Q U I E T G P Y T H S P E C T K T M J L
G L I E S O C O A F S H V N N I P E M
Y H V R G T I X T F T H Q E E Y S H W K
F P A B L D N B O H R N H L T G S H S S
V I D N A P E O P L E I O S A U S G E
D J Z R D L P I J R D K C V D B Z B Q J
S T I L L I D I A R Y C H A P A P E R
```

AFRICA	DIPHTHERIA	JEWS	MUMMY	SAUSAGE
AMSTERDAM	DUSSEL	KISS	OTTO	SECRET
ANNEXE	ELLIE	KITTY	PAPER	STAR
BURGLARS	FRANK	KOLEN	PEOPLE	STILL
CAKE	GESTAPO	KRALER	POTATOES	STUDY
CAMPS	GHANDI	LIES	QUARREL	TRAINS
CLOTHES	HENK	LOVE	QUIET	WESTERBORK
CUPBOARD	HITLER	MARGOT	RADIO	
DENTIST	HOLLAND	MEIP	RAID	
DIARY	ITALY	MOUSCHI	RAUTER	

Anne Frank Word Search 3 Answer Key

AFRICA	DIPHTHERIA	JEWS	MUMMY	SAUSAGE
AMSTERDAM	DUSSEL	KISS	OTTO	SECRET
ANNEXE	ELLIE	KITTY	PAPER	STAR
BURGLARS	FRANK	KOLEN	PEOPLE	STILL
CAKE	GESTAPO	KRALER	POTATOES	STUDY
CAMPS	GHANDI	LIES	QUARREL	TRAINS
CLOTHES	HENK	LOVE	QUIET	WESTERBORK
CUPBOARD	HITLER	MARGOT	RADIO	
DENTIST	HOLLAND	MEIP	RAID	
DIARY	ITALY	MOUSCHI	RAUTER	

Anne Frank Word Search 4

```
K R A L E R S T I L L M Y T H O L O G Y
D A K F E P O S E I V E J J R R Q T K Z
Z I D T G G A S C E D P T W L A U I R
P D U C R L S S Z S D F E T J J I O S L
D A W A Y U G H A N D I R Q E S E N S H
R I M K D M I E A U N L C A U R T W S B
A R K E S T B H S S S D E B N A S U S B
O E V O L T T Y O T Z A S K Z K R M D P
B H C E J R A Z I G A B G N C C J R S Y
P T R S O Y A R D E L P O E P B Q K E T
U H D H M M F F A J B Z O H V S J O H L
C P S J O F U F R A N K F O R T S O T Q
C I S R U L H M P I K R E P A P N P S C
R D S C S V L H M G C O Y D M M X H L C
M J W H C D I A R Y X A L A M M E U C T
B I R T H D A Y N L G J C E E L L I E B
W K F K I T T Y H D E X E N N A G S P V
X V B U R G L A R S Z D E N T I S T Z W
```

AFRICA	DIPHTHERIA	ITALY	MARGOT	RADIO
ANNEXE	DUSSEL	JEWS	MEIP	RAID
BIRTHDAY	ELLIE	KISS	MOUSCHI	RAUTER
BURGLARS	FRANK	KITTY	MUMMY	SAUSAGE
CAKE	FRANKFORT	KOLEN	MYTHOLOGY	SECRET
CAMPS	GESTAPO	KOOPHUIS	OTTO	SHORTHAND
CLOTHES	GHANDI	KRALER	PAPER	STAR
CUPBOARD	HENK	LETTERS	PEOPLE	STILL
DENTIST	HITLER	LIES	QUARREL	STUDY
DIARY	HOLLAND	LOVE	QUIET	TRAINS

Copyrighted

Anne Frank Word Search 4 Answer Key

AFRICA	DIPHTHERIA	ITALY	MARGOT	RADIO
ANNEXE	DUSSEL	JEWS	MEIP	RAID
BIRTHDAY	ELLIE	KISS	MOUSCHI	RAUTER
BURGLARS	FRANK	KITTY	MUMMY	SAUSAGE
CAKE	FRANKFORT	KOLEN	MYTHOLOGY	SECRET
CAMPS	GESTAPO	KOOPHUIS	OTTO	SHORTHAND
CLOTHES	GHANDI	KRALER	PAPER	STAR
CUPBOARD	HENK	LETTERS	PEOPLE	STILL
DENTIST	HITLER	LIES	QUARREL	STUDY
DIARY	HOLLAND	LOVE	QUIET	TRAINS

Anne Frank Crossword 1

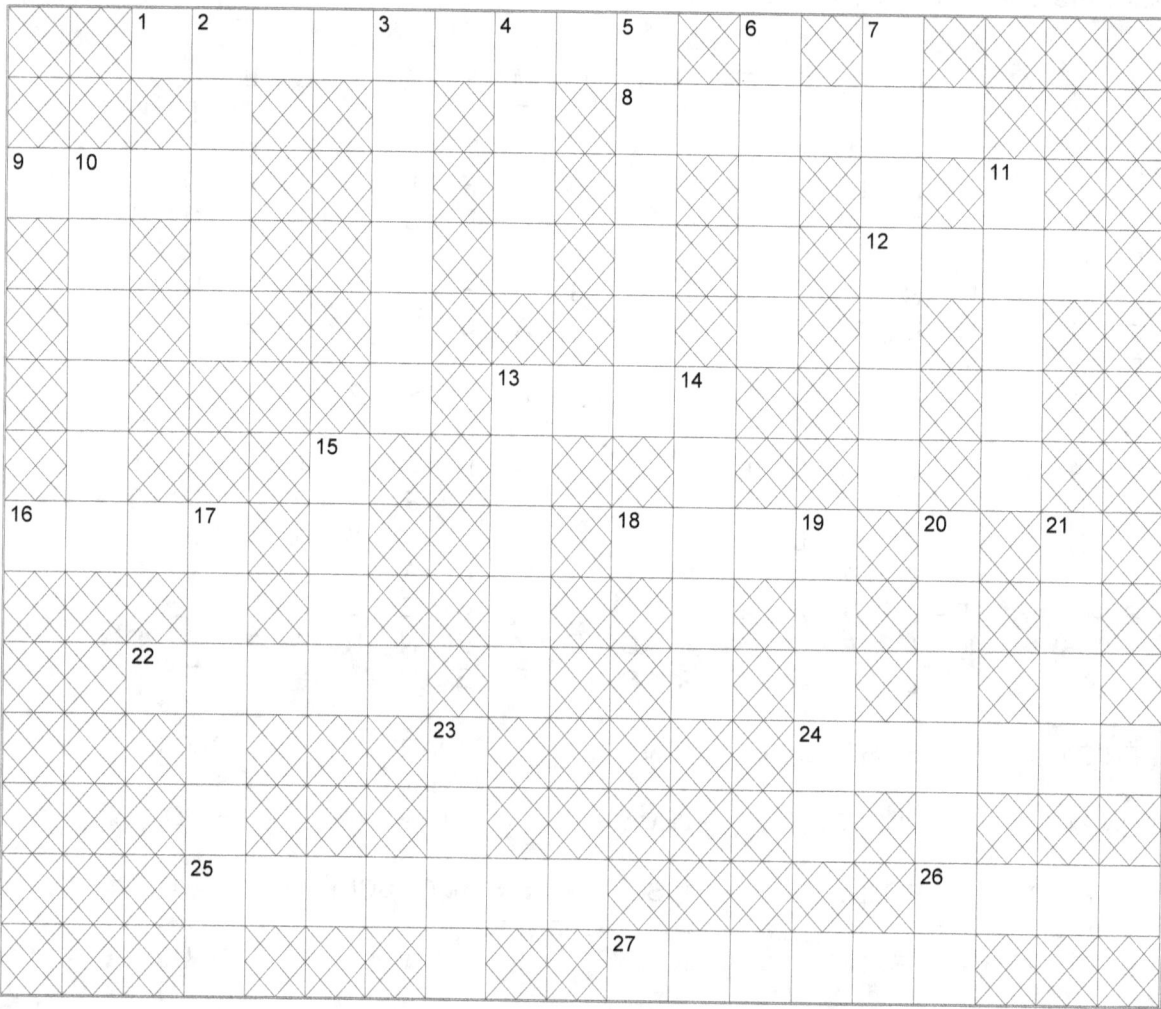

Across
1. City of Anne's birth
8. German 'big shot' in Holland; Anne mentions his speech
9. Air _____; bombing
12. Henk's wife; office worker; brought news & presents
13. Peter & Anne have a 'goodnight' ____
16. Hitler wanted to exterminate all of them
18. Anne saw her pleading, 'Help, oh, help me . . .'
22. Making no sounds
24. Elderly dentist who shares Anne's room
25. German secret police who came for the Jews
26. Meip's husband
27. Freedom-loving, pacifist revolutionary in India

Down
2. Clandestine 'source of courage'
3. Assumed Mr. Frank's business responsibilities
4. Mr. Frank
5. Public transportation from which Jews were banned
6. Mrs. Frank
7. Country of Anne's birth
10. Secret ____
11. Anne's personal notebook
13. Anne's fictitious diary friend
14. Making no movements
15. Feeling Anne has for Peter
17. Mr. VanDaan made meat into this
19. Anne loved to read & _____ to pass the time
20. Peter's cat
21. Edible Christmas present with 'Peace 1944' written on it
23. Yellow ornament Jews had to wear

Anne Frank Crossword 1 Answer Key

		1 F	2 R	A	N	3 K	F	4 O	R	5 T		6 M		7 G				
			A			R		T		8 R	A	U	T	E	R			
9 R	10 A	I	D			A		T		A		M		R		11 D		
	N		I			L		O		I		M		12 M	E	I	P	
	N		O			E				N		Y		A		A		
	E					R		13 K	I	S	14 S			N		R		
	X				15 L			I			T			Y		Y		
16 J	E	W	17 S		O			T		18 L	I	E	19 S		20 M		21 C	
			A		V			T			L		T		O		A	
		22 Q	U	I	E	T		Y			L		U		U		K	
			S				23 S						24 D	U	S	S	E	L
			A				T						Y		C			
			25 G	E	S	T	A	P	O						26 H	E	N	K
			E				R			27 G	H	A	N	D	I			

Across
1. City of Anne's birth
8. German 'big shot' in Holland; Anne mentions his speech
9. Air _____; bombing
12. Henk's wife; office worker; brought news & presents
13. Peter & Anne have a 'goodnight' ____
16. Hitler wanted to exterminate all of them
18. Anne saw her pleading, 'Help, oh, help me . . .'
22. Making no sounds
24. Elderly dentist who shares Anne's room
25. German secret police who came for the Jews
26. Meip's husband
27. Freedom-loving, pacifist revolutionary in India

Down
2. Clandestine 'source of courage'
3. Assumed Mr. Frank's business responsibilities
4. Mr. Frank
5. Public transportation from which Jews were banned
6. Mrs. Frank
7. Country of Anne's birth
10. Secret ____
11. Anne's personal notebook
13. Anne's fictitious diary friend
14. Making no movements
15. Feeling Anne has for Peter
17. Mr. VanDaan made meat into this
19. Anne loved to read & _____ to pass the time
20. Peter's cat
21. Edible Christmas present with 'Peace 1944' written on it
23. Yellow ornament Jews had to wear

Anne Frank Crossword 2

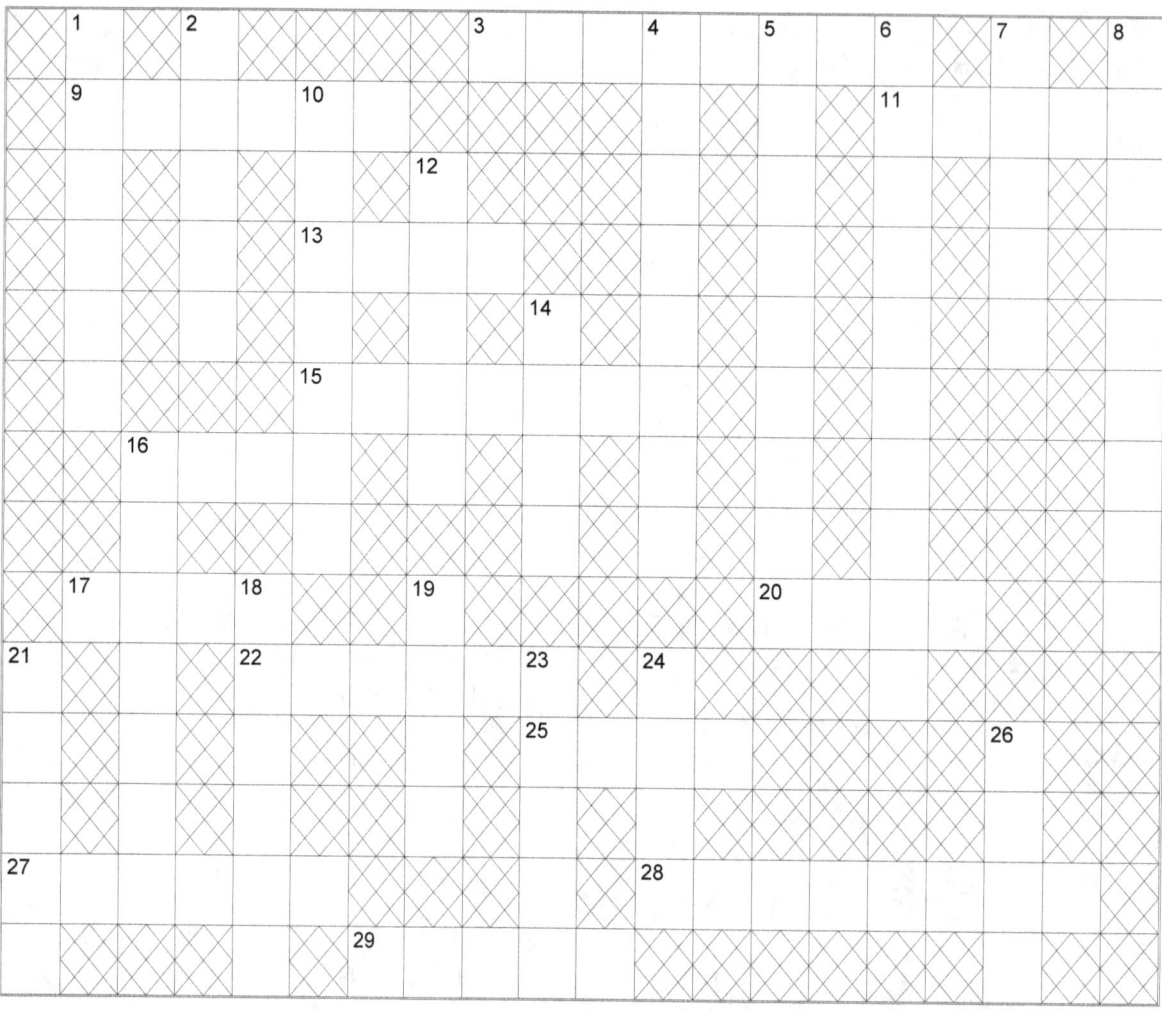

Across

3. Secret entrance to the annexe
9. Continent allied forces invaded in 1942
11. It 'capitulated' in September 1943
13. Mr. Frank
15. Country to which the Franks moved in 1933
16. Feeling Anne has for Peter
17. Yellow ornament Jews had to wear
20. Henk's wife; office worker; brought news & presents
22. Secret ____
25. Anne saw her pleading, 'Help, oh, help me . . .'
27. Elderly dentist who shares Anne's room
28. He was especially helpful in arranging logistics & getting food
29. Making no sounds

Down

1. Anne's sister
2. Anne's last name
4. Day Anne's diary starts
5. City where the Secret Annexe was located
6. Sickness in Eli's home that kept her away for 6 weeks
7. Clandestine 'source of courage'
8. Study of Greek & Roman gods
10. Anne's & Margo's were shabby & too small
12. Making no movements
14. Edible Christmas present with 'Peace 1944' written on it
16. Anne wrote them to Margot and her father
18. German 'big shot' in Holland; Anne mentions his speech
19. Hitler wanted to exterminate all of them
21. Anne loved to read & _____ to pass the time
23. She & Meip help keep spirits up in the annexe
24. Meip's husband
26. Air _____; bombing

Anne Frank Crossword 2 Answer Key

	1 M	2 F		3 C	4 U	5 P	6 B	7 O	8 A	R	D		R		M
9	A	F	R	I	C	A			I		M	11 I	T	A	L	Y
	R	A		L			12 S		R		S		P		D		T
	G	N		13 O	T	T	O		T		T		H		I		H
	O	K		T		I		14 C	H		E		T		O		O
	T			15 H	O	L	L	A	N	D		R		H		L
		16 L	O	V	E		L		K		A		D		E		O
		E				S			E		Y		A		R		G
		17 S	T	18 A	R		19 J				20 M	E	I	P		Y
21 S		T		22 A	N	N	E	X	23 E		24 H				A		
T		E		U			W		25 L	I	E	S				26 R	
U		R		T			S		L		N					A	
27 D	U	S	S	E	L				I		28 K	O	O	P	H	U	I	S
Y						29 R	Q	U	I	E	T					D	

Across
- 3. Secret entrance to the annexe
- 9. Continent allied forces invaded in 1942
- 11. It 'capitulated' in September 1943
- 13. Mr. Frank
- 15. Country to which the Franks moved in 1933
- 16. Feeling Anne has for Peter
- 17. Yellow ornament Jews had to wear
- 20. Henk's wife; office worker; brought news & presents
- 22. Secret ____
- 25. Anne saw her pleading, 'Help, oh, help me . . .'
- 27. Elderly dentist who shares Anne's room
- 28. He was especially helpful in arranging logistics & getting food
- 29. Making no sounds

Down
- 1. Anne's sister
- 2. Anne's last name
- 4. Day Anne's diary starts
- 5. City where the Secret Annexe was located
- 6. Sickness in Eli's home that kept her away for 6 weeks
- 7. Clandestine 'source of courage'
- 8. Study of Greek & Roman gods
- 10. Anne's & Margo's were shabby & too small
- 12. Making no movements
- 14. Edible Christmas present with 'Peace 1944' written on it
- 16. Anne wrote them to Margot and her father
- 18. German 'big shot' in Holland; Anne mentions his speech
- 19. Hitler wanted to exterminate all of them
- 21. Anne loved to read & _____ to pass the time
- 23. She & Meip help keep spirits up in the annexe
- 24. Meip's husband
- 26. Air _____; bombing

41
Copyrighted

Anne Frank Crossword 3

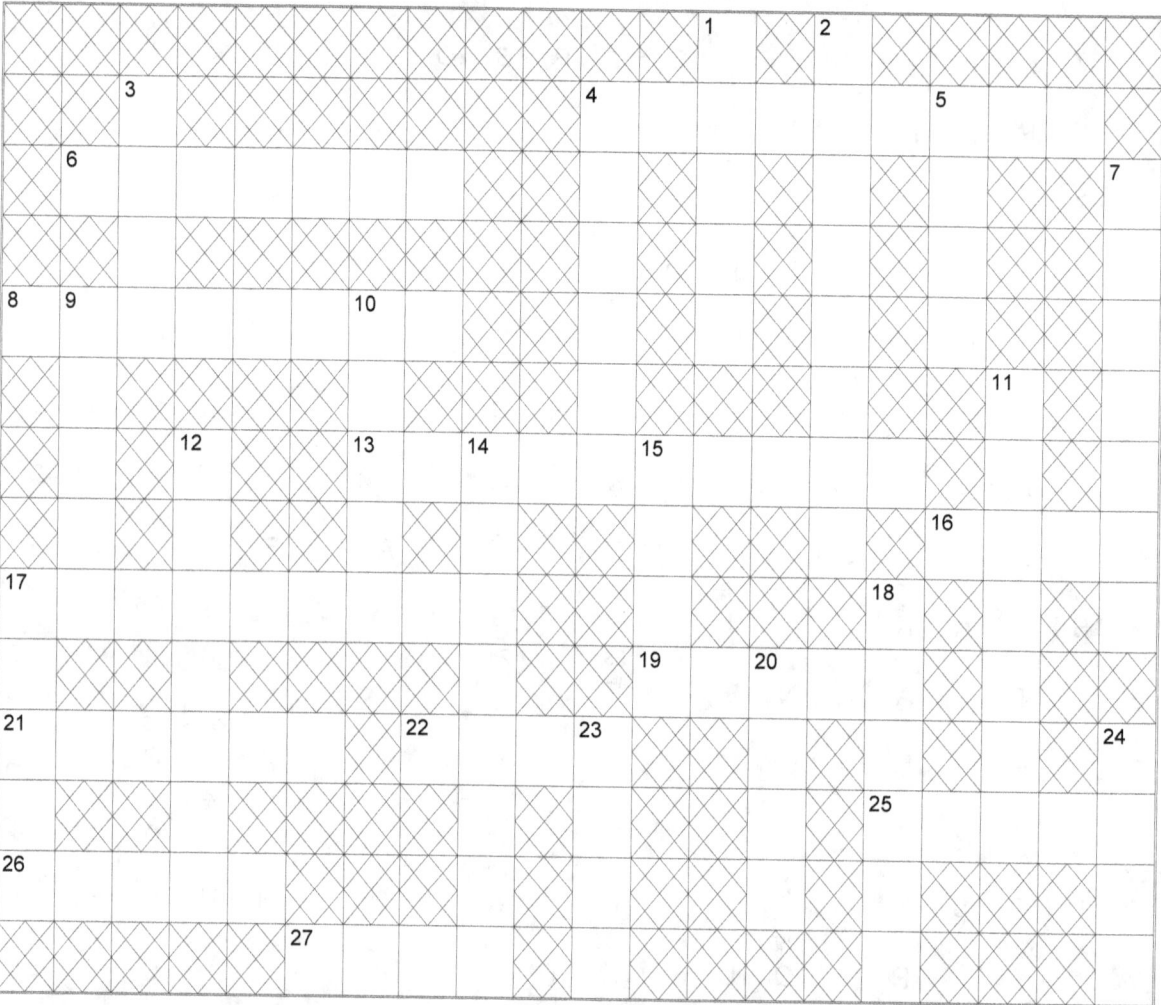

Across
4. Study of Greek & Roman gods
6. Anne wrote them to Margot and her father
8. Place where Anne & Peter meet in the evenings
13. Sickness in Eli's home that kept her away for 6 weeks
16. Edible Christmas present with 'Peace 1944' written on it
17. City of Anne's birth
19. ___ and Co.; firm in which Mr. Frank was a partner
21. Continent allied forces invaded in 1942
22. Yellow ornament Jews had to wear
25. She & Meip help keep spirits up in the annexe
26. Anne's fictitious diary friend
27. Anne saw her pleading, 'Help, oh, help me . . .'

Down
1. Making no movements
2. He was especially helpful in arranging logistics & getting food
3. Hitler wanted to exterminate all of them
4. Anne's sister
5. Mr. Frank
7. Anne's & Margo's were shabby & too small
9. It is more patient than man
10. Clandestine 'source of courage'
11. Verbal fight
12. Dussel's occupation
14. Staple vegetable at the annexe
15. Meip's husband
17. Anne's last name
18. Secret ____
20. Feeling Anne has for Peter
23. Air _____; bombing
24. Henk's wife; office worker; brought news & presents

Anne Frank Crossword 3 Answer Key

								1 S	2 K			
	3 J				4 M	Y	T	H	O	5 L	O	G	Y
6 L	E	T	T	E	R	S	A		I		O		T		7 C
	W				R		L		P		T		L
8 U	9 P	S	T	10 A	I	R	S	G		L		H		O		O
	A			A			O				U	11 Q		T
	P	12 D		13 D	14 I	P	H	T	15 H	E	R	I	A			H
	E	E		I				O		E		S	16 C	A	K	E
17 F	R	A	N	K	F	O	R	T		N			18 A		R		S
R		T						A		19 K	20 O	L	E	N		R
21 A	F	R	I	C	A		22 S	T	23 A	R			O		N		E	24 M
N		S							O				V	25 E	L	L	I	E
26 K	I	T	T	Y					I				E	X				I
					27 L	I	E	S		D				E				P

Across
- 4. Study of Greek & Roman gods
- 6. Anne wrote them to Margot and her father
- 8. Place where Anne & Peter meet in the evenings
- 13. Sickness in Eli's home that kept her away for 6 weeks
- 16. Edible Christmas present with 'Peace 1944' written on it
- 17. City of Anne's birth
- 19. ___ and Co.; firm in which Mr. Frank was a partner
- 21. Continent allied forces invaded in 1942
- 22. Yellow ornament Jews had to wear
- 25. She & Meip help keep spirits up in the annexe
- 26. Anne's fictitious diary friend
- 27. Anne saw her pleading, 'Help, oh, help me . . .'
- 7. Anne's & Margo's were shabby & too small
- 9. It is more patient than man
- 10. Clandestine 'source of courage'
- 11. Verbal fight
- 12. Dussel's occupation
- 14. Staple vegetable at the annexe
- 15. Meip's husband
- 17. Anne's last name
- 18. Secret ____
- 20. Feeling Anne has for Peter
- 23. Air _____; bombing
- 24. Henk's wife; office worker; brought news & presents

Down
- 1. Making no movements
- 2. He was especially helpful in arranging logistics & getting food
- 3. Hitler wanted to exterminate all of them
- 4. Anne's sister
- 5. Mr. Frank

Anne Frank Crossword 4

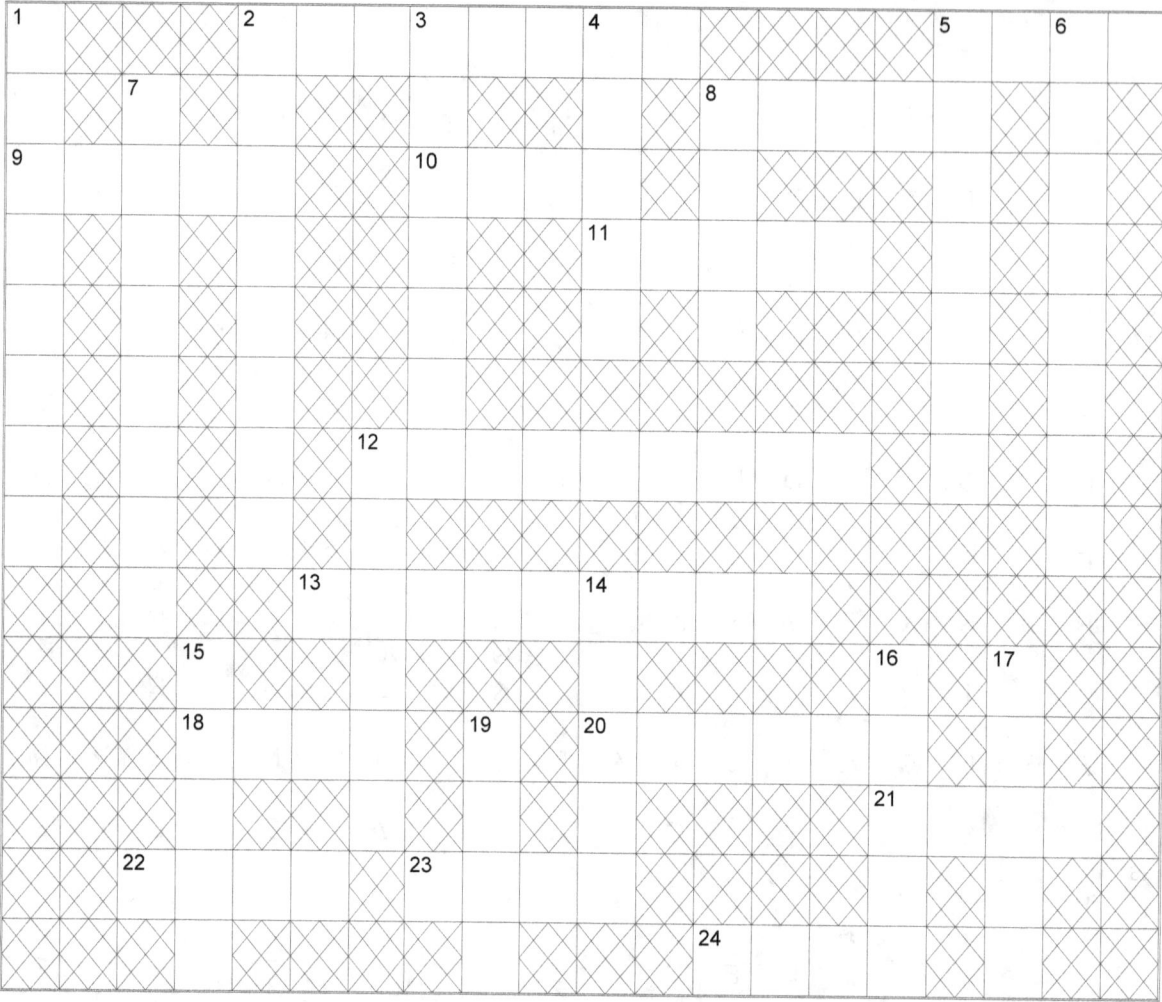

Across
2. They took cashboxes, sugar coupons & more
5. Edible Christmas present with 'Peace 1944' written on it
8. Making no movements
9. It is more patient than man
10. Air _____; bombing
11. It 'capitulated' in September 1943
12. Study of Greek & Roman gods
13. City of Anne's birth
18. Mr. Frank
20. Continent allied forces invaded in 1942
21. Henk's wife; office worker; brought news & presents
22. Hitler wanted to exterminate all of them
23. Meip's husband
24. Peter & Anne have a 'goodnight' ____

6. He was especially helpful in arranging logistics & getting food
7. Place where Anne & Peter meet in the evenings
8. Yellow ornament Jews had to wear
12. Anne's sister
14. Anne's last name
15. ___ and Co.; firm in which Mr. Frank was a partner
16. Concentration _____
17. Making no sounds
19. Anne saw her pleading, 'Help, oh, help me . . .'

Down
1. Secret entrance to the annexe
2. Day Anne's diary starts
3. Country of Anne's birth
4. Clandestine 'source of courage'
5. Anne's & Margo's were shabby & too small

Anne Frank Crossword 4 Answer Key

	1 C		2 B	U	R	3 G	L	4 A	R	S		5 C	A	6 K	E
	U		7 U	I		E		A		8 S	T	I	L	L	O
9 P	A	P	E	R		10 R	A	I	D		T		O		O
	B		S	T		M			11 I	T	A	L	Y		P
	O		T	H		A			O		R			H		H
	A		A	D		N		12 M	Y	T	H	O	L	O	G	Y	S		I
	R		I	A				A									S
	D		R	Y				A							
			S		13 F	R	A	N	K	14 F	O	R	T	
			15 K		G			R				16 C		17 Q
			18 O	T	T	O		19 L		20 A	F	R	I	C	A		U
			L		T			I		N				21 M	E	I	P
		22 J	E	W	S		23 H	E	N	K			P		E
			N				S			24 K	I	S	S		T

Across

2. They took cashboxes, sugar coupons & more
5. Edible Christmas present with 'Peace 1944' written on it
8. Making no movements
9. It is more patient than man
10. Air _____; bombing
11. It 'capitulated' in September 1943
12. Study of Greek & Roman gods
13. City of Anne's birth
18. Mr. Frank
20. Continent allied forces invaded in 1942
21. Henk's wife; office worker; brought news & presents
22. Hitler wanted to exterminate all of them
23. Meip's husband
24. Peter & Anne have a 'goodnight' ____

Down

1. Secret entrance to the annexe
2. Day Anne's diary starts
3. Country of Anne's birth
4. Clandestine 'source of courage'
5. Anne's & Margo's were shabby & too small
6. He was especially helpful in arranging logistics & getting food
7. Place where Anne & Peter meet in the evenings
8. Yellow ornament Jews had to wear
12. Anne's sister
14. Anne's last name
15. ___ and Co.; firm in which Mr. Frank was a partner
16. Concentration _____
17. Making no sounds
19. Anne saw her pleading, 'Help, oh, help me . . .'

Anne Frank

KISS	ANNEXE	SAUSAGE	ITALY	LIES
OTTO	JEWS	STAR	CLOTHES	HENK
MARGOT	RAUTER	FREE SPACE	HOLLAND	TRAINS
LOVE	WESTERBORK	DIPHTHERIA	GERMANY	SECRET
QUARREL	MUMMY	KITTY	MYTHOLOGY	AFRICA

Anne Frank

CAKE	STILL	BURGLARS	PAPER	BIRTHDAY
GHANDI	HITLER	DENTIST	SHORTHAND	CUPBOARD
DUSSEL	PEOPLE	FREE SPACE	FRANK	CAMPS
MOUSCHI	ELLIE	KOOPHUIS	DIARY	UPSTAIRS
KRALER	RADIO	LETTERS	VANDAANS	STUDY

Anne Frank

HENK	PAPER	POTATOES	RAID	UPSTAIRS
CAMPS	ANNEXE	AMSTERDAM	KISS	HOLLAND
ITALY	GHANDI	FREE SPACE	CUPBOARD	HITLER
KOOPHUIS	DIPHTHERIA	CLOTHES	FRANK	BURGLARS
OTTO	SECRET	TRAINS	RADIO	DIARY

Anne Frank

AFRICA	WESTERBORK	MEIP	DENTIST	BIRTHDAY
JEWS	CAKE	SAUSAGE	GERMANY	GESTAPO
LOVE	VANDAANS	FREE SPACE	SHORTHAND	LIES
KOLEN	KITTY	LETTERS	MUMMY	PEOPLE
DUSSEL	FRANKFORT	QUIET	ELLIE	MOUSCHI

Anne Frank

OTTO	QUIET	CAMPS	MOUSCHI	AFRICA
VANDAANS	BIRTHDAY	CLOTHES	RAUTER	KISS
ITALY	QUARREL	FREE SPACE	HITLER	MEIP
KRALER	PEOPLE	SECRET	MYTHOLOGY	WESTERBORK
CAKE	LIES	MARGOT	BURGLARS	STAR

Anne Frank

HENK	DUSSEL	DIPHTHERIA	MUMMY	GHANDI
DENTIST	STUDY	LOVE	RADIO	ANNEXE
GERMANY	DIARY	FREE SPACE	LETTERS	FRANK
JEWS	SHORTHAND	TRAINS	KOLEN	FRANKFORT
STILL	GESTAPO	SAUSAGE	AMSTERDAM	PAPER

Anne Frank

RAUTER	BIRTHDAY	HENK	STILL	CAKE
LIES	STAR	WESTERBORK	POTATOES	JEWS
ELLIE	MOUSCHI	FREE SPACE	DUSSEL	TRAINS
KITTY	SECRET	KOLEN	ITALY	HITLER
FRANKFORT	AMSTERDAM	MYTHOLOGY	VANDAANS	DIARY

Anne Frank

QUARREL	CAMPS	PAPER	FRANK	GERMANY
PEOPLE	MUMMY	QUIET	KOOPHUIS	LETTERS
CUPBOARD	UPSTAIRS	FREE SPACE	OTTO	MARGOT
KRALER	DIPHTHERIA	RADIO	DENTIST	LOVE
KISS	SAUSAGE	AFRICA	BURGLARS	RAID

Anne Frank

GHANDI	GESTAPO	MYTHOLOGY	HOLLAND	SAUSAGE
SECRET	LIES	KITTY	DIARY	CAKE
DENTIST	BIRTHDAY	FREE SPACE	POTATOES	ELLIE
BURGLARS	RAUTER	MARGOT	GERMANY	KISS
WESTERBORK	ANNEXE	CLOTHES	MOUSCHI	KRALER

Anne Frank

DIPHTHERIA	LETTERS	HITLER	ITALY	VANDAANS
MEIP	AMSTERDAM	DUSSEL	PEOPLE	JEWS
PAPER	TRAINS	FREE SPACE	FRANKFORT	HENK
OTTO	QUARREL	STILL	UPSTAIRS	MUMMY
LOVE	AFRICA	CAMPS	RADIO	STUDY

Anne Frank

UPSTAIRS	QUARREL	CAKE	RADIO	QUIET
HITLER	RAID	KITTY	GESTAPO	STILL
DIARY	PEOPLE	FREE SPACE	WESTERBORK	SHORTHAND
LIES	MYTHOLOGY	DIPHTHERIA	HENK	GHANDI
MOUSCHI	CAMPS	MEIP	DENTIST	BURGLARS

Anne Frank

STUDY	JEWS	TRAINS	KISS	STAR
MARGOT	KOLEN	VANDAANS	MUMMY	SECRET
POTATOES	ITALY	FREE SPACE	HOLLAND	BIRTHDAY
CLOTHES	LETTERS	CUPBOARD	PAPER	AFRICA
ANNEXE	ELLIE	KOOPHUIS	FRANK	KRALER

Anne Frank

PAPER	KISS	KRALER	CAKE	ITALY
BURGLARS	MEIP	MOUSCHI	UPSTAIRS	VANDAANS
GESTAPO	CLOTHES	FREE SPACE	CUPBOARD	QUARREL
FRANK	CAMPS	FRANKFORT	GERMANY	RAID
STUDY	DIPHTHERIA	MARGOT	WESTERBORK	POTATOES

Anne Frank

LETTERS	ANNEXE	RADIO	KOOPHUIS	DIARY
AMSTERDAM	SAUSAGE	SECRET	MUMMY	STILL
MYTHOLOGY	QUIET	FREE SPACE	BIRTHDAY	LOVE
AFRICA	OTTO	HOLLAND	HITLER	TRAINS
DENTIST	DUSSEL	STAR	HENK	GHANDI

Anne Frank

ANNEXE	MYTHOLOGY	CUPBOARD	GESTAPO	CAKE
RADIO	DENTIST	BIRTHDAY	KOLEN	OTTO
FRANKFORT	FRANK	FREE SPACE	AMSTERDAM	SECRET
STAR	DIARY	HITLER	LETTERS	KISS
POTATOES	QUARREL	STUDY	KOOPHUIS	KITTY

Anne Frank

PEOPLE	HOLLAND	VANDAANS	MOUSCHI	MEIP
ELLIE	SHORTHAND	WESTERBORK	GERMANY	DUSSEL
BURGLARS	SAUSAGE	FREE SPACE	RAID	CLOTHES
AFRICA	LIES	GHANDI	MUMMY	LOVE
DIPHTHERIA	HENK	STILL	RAUTER	QUIET

Anne Frank

JEWS	GERMANY	UPSTAIRS	RAUTER	STILL
STUDY	LOVE	SHORTHAND	MEIP	ANNEXE
CLOTHES	QUARREL	FREE SPACE	GESTAPO	STAR
HITLER	TRAINS	CUPBOARD	QUIET	KOLEN
BURGLARS	SAUSAGE	KRALER	WESTERBORK	PEOPLE

Anne Frank

FRANK	LIES	MARGOT	OTTO	SECRET
MYTHOLOGY	KITTY	ITALY	HOLLAND	DUSSEL
AMSTERDAM	DENTIST	FREE SPACE	KOOPHUIS	HENK
AFRICA	FRANKFORT	BIRTHDAY	DIPHTHERIA	LETTERS
MUMMY	GHANDI	POTATOES	MOUSCHI	KISS

Anne Frank

KITTY	MYTHOLOGY	TRAINS	LOVE	JEWS
ELLIE	VANDAANS	OTTO	KOLEN	MOUSCHI
MEIP	QUARREL	FREE SPACE	CLOTHES	PEOPLE
STUDY	STAR	KISS	FRANKFORT	KOOPHUIS
UPSTAIRS	GHANDI	LIES	GESTAPO	MARGOT

Anne Frank

STILL	RAUTER	PAPER	ANNEXE	DIPHTHERIA
HOLLAND	LETTERS	KRALER	FRANK	RAID
HENK	CUPBOARD	FREE SPACE	AMSTERDAM	BIRTHDAY
MUMMY	WESTERBORK	RADIO	SAUSAGE	HITLER
ITALY	SECRET	POTATOES	QUIET	DENTIST

Anne Frank

WESTERBORK	PAPER	MUMMY	VANDAANS	KOLEN
UPSTAIRS	BIRTHDAY	SECRET	KISS	FRANKFORT
GERMANY	KITTY	FREE SPACE	BURGLARS	RAID
SAUSAGE	LOVE	DIPHTHERIA	DUSSEL	LETTERS
PEOPLE	MARGOT	LIES	HENK	RADIO

Anne Frank

CUPBOARD	STUDY	ELLIE	KRALER	QUIET
AMSTERDAM	AFRICA	TRAINS	MEIP	SHORTHAND
CAMPS	HITLER	FREE SPACE	FRANK	STILL
QUARREL	POTATOES	ITALY	RAUTER	CAKE
GESTAPO	HOLLAND	STAR	GHANDI	DIARY

Anne Frank

MYTHOLOGY	DIARY	OTTO	KOOPHUIS	QUARREL
LETTERS	BURGLARS	STAR	STILL	HENK
WESTERBORK	LIES	FREE SPACE	POTATOES	CUPBOARD
STUDY	DENTIST	CAKE	KRALER	BIRTHDAY
VANDAANS	PAPER	ELLIE	CAMPS	RAID

Anne Frank

ITALY	FRANK	LOVE	GHANDI	TRAINS
RADIO	RAUTER	MUMMY	QUIET	AMSTERDAM
DUSSEL	CLOTHES	FREE SPACE	HOLLAND	UPSTAIRS
HITLER	MEIP	FRANKFORT	AFRICA	KOLEN
DIPHTHERIA	KITTY	GESTAPO	KISS	JEWS

Anne Frank

SHORTHAND	ANNEXE	HENK	ITALY	GERMANY
AFRICA	MOUSCHI	MYTHOLOGY	OTTO	ELLIE
TRAINS	JEWS	FREE SPACE	DIARY	DUSSEL
STAR	CLOTHES	FRANK	MARGOT	CUPBOARD
DIPHTHERIA	RAID	CAKE	LETTERS	GHANDI

Anne Frank

HOLLAND	VANDAANS	MEIP	KITTY	AMSTERDAM
MUMMY	POTATOES	LIES	UPSTAIRS	SAUSAGE
BURGLARS	WESTERBORK	FREE SPACE	FRANKFORT	PAPER
BIRTHDAY	RADIO	GESTAPO	STILL	QUIET
CAMPS	PEOPLE	RAUTER	SECRET	DENTIST

Anne Frank

KOLEN	KITTY	QUIET	ITALY	HENK
MUMMY	GERMANY	ELLIE	RADIO	HITLER
UPSTAIRS	DUSSEL	FREE SPACE	GESTAPO	GHANDI
CUPBOARD	CAKE	PEOPLE	DIARY	JEWS
FRANKFORT	DENTIST	CAMPS	KOOPHUIS	KRALER

Anne Frank

LIES	HOLLAND	PAPER	AFRICA	VANDAANS
ANNEXE	STAR	AMSTERDAM	BIRTHDAY	STILL
RAUTER	WESTERBORK	FREE SPACE	TRAINS	QUARREL
STUDY	LETTERS	SHORTHAND	BURGLARS	DIPHTHERIA
SECRET	RAID	MOUSCHI	FRANK	LOVE

Anne Frank

PAPER	KOLEN	ITALY	BURGLARS	FRANK
KITTY	BIRTHDAY	MUMMY	AMSTERDAM	UPSTAIRS
QUIET	RAUTER	FREE SPACE	GERMANY	PEOPLE
MYTHOLOGY	STILL	SHORTHAND	LOVE	DENTIST
WESTERBORK	KRALER	FRANKFORT	CAMPS	POTATOES

Anne Frank

MOUSCHI	SECRET	SAUSAGE	DIPHTHERIA	KOOPHUIS
TRAINS	ELLIE	KISS	MARGOT	RAID
LIES	QUARREL	FREE SPACE	DIARY	JEWS
DUSSEL	CAKE	RADIO	CUPBOARD	HOLLAND
HITLER	STUDY	OTTO	GHANDI	AFRICA

Anne Frank

GERMANY	GHANDI	PEOPLE	RAID	SHORTHAND
DIARY	UPSTAIRS	HOLLAND	MEIP	MARGOT
CAMPS	STILL	FREE SPACE	DUSSEL	QUIET
QUARREL	MYTHOLOGY	VANDAANS	OTTO	KITTY
STUDY	DENTIST	LIES	TRAINS	DIPHTHERIA

Anne Frank

RAUTER	HENK	KISS	JEWS	FRANKFORT
STAR	LETTERS	LOVE	GESTAPO	POTATOES
HITLER	MOUSCHI	FREE SPACE	AMSTERDAM	MUMMY
RADIO	CLOTHES	KRALER	WESTERBORK	BIRTHDAY
KOLEN	BURGLARS	SAUSAGE	CUPBOARD	SECRET

Anne Frank Vocabulary Word List

No.	Word	Clue/Definition
1.	ADO	Bustle; fuss; bother
2.	ADROIT	Skillful and adept under pressure
3.	ALOOF	Reserved; remote
4.	ARDENT	Fervent; passionate
5.	BLISS	Extreme happiness
6.	BOISTEROUS	Loud; lacking in restraint or discipline
7.	CAPITULATION	Surrender under specified conditions
8.	CHATTELS	Personal, movable property
9.	CLANDESTINE	Kept secret to conceal an improper purpose
10.	COMPENSATION	Offset; counterbalance; repayment
11.	CONCEITED	Characterized by holding an unusually high opinion of oneself
12.	CONDOLE	To express sympathy
13.	CONGENIAL	Friendly
14.	COQUETTISH	Characteristic of a woman who makes teasing romantic overtures
15.	DIN	Jumble of loud noises
16.	DISDAINFUL	Despicable; contemptible
17.	FANATIC	Person with an extreme enthusiasm for something
18.	FATALIST	One who believes all events are predetermined and inevitable
19.	FATUOUS	Foolish
20.	IMMORTAL	Never to be forgotten
21.	IMPERTINENT	Improperly forward or bold
22.	INCESSANTLY	Continually, without interruption
23.	INEVITABLY	Unavoidably
24.	LIBERATED	Freed
25.	LOATHE	Hate; extreme dislike
26.	MANIFEST	Show plainly; reveal
27.	NUISANCE	Bother
28.	OBSTINATE	Stubborn
29.	OPPRESSIVE	Difficult to bear; weighing heavily on the spirit
30.	PALL	To become dull or boring
31.	PERPLEXED	Troubled with uncertainty
32.	PIQUED	Provoked; full of resentment
33.	PLIED	Assailed
34.	PRIVATIONS	Lack of basic necessities of life
35.	PROCURED	Got by special effort; obtained
36.	PROFICIENT	Adept; expert
37.	PRUDE	One who is excessively concerned with being proper
38.	PSEUDONYM	A fictitious name used by an author
39.	QUEERLY	Oddly
40.	REBUKE	Reprimand; criticize
41.	SARCASM	Cutting remarks
42.	SCOFFINGLY	Mockingly
43.	SHAMMING	Putting on a false appearance
44.	SOLE	Only
45.	SUPERFLUOUS	Not needed
46.	TACT	Ability to act or speak without offending
47.	TINGE	Slight addition
48.	TOLERANT	Inclined to put up with beliefs, practices or traits of others
49.	UNASSUMING	Modest
50.	VAGUE	Not clearly expressed; inexplicit

Anne Frank Vocabulary Fill In The Blank 1

_____ 1. Only

_____ 2. Loud; lacking in restraint or discipline

_____ 3. Characterized by holding an unusually high opinion of oneself

_____ 4. One who believes all events are predetermined and inevitable

_____ 5. Oddly

_____ 6. Reserved; remote

_____ 7. Never to be forgotten

_____ 8. Bustle; fuss; bother

_____ 9. Stubborn

_____ 10. Friendly

_____ 11. Skillful and adept under pressure

_____ 12. Offset; counterbalance; repayment

_____ 13. Slight addition

_____ 14. Person with an extreme enthusiasm for something

_____ 15. Modest

_____ 16. Got by special effort; obtained

_____ 17. A fictitious name used by an author

_____ 18. Foolish

_____ 19. One who is excessively concerned with being proper

_____ 20. Extreme happiness

Anne Frank Vocabulary Fill In The Blank 1 Answer Key

SOLE	1. Only
BOISTEROUS	2. Loud; lacking in restraint or discipline
CONCEITED	3. Characterized by holding an unusually high opinion of oneself
FATALIST	4. One who believes all events are predetermined and inevitable
QUEERLY	5. Oddly
ALOOF	6. Reserved; remote
IMMORTAL	7. Never to be forgotten
ADO	8. Bustle; fuss; bother
OBSTINATE	9. Stubborn
CONGENIAL	10. Friendly
ADROIT	11. Skillful and adept under pressure
COMPENSATION	12. Offset; counterbalance; repayment
TINGE	13. Slight addition
FANATIC	14. Person with an extreme enthusiasm for something
UNASSUMING	15. Modest
PROCURED	16. Got by special effort; obtained
PSEUDONYM	17. A fictitious name used by an author
FATUOUS	18. Foolish
PRUDE	19. One who is excessively concerned with being proper
BLISS	20. Extreme happiness

Anne Frank Vocabulary Fill In The Blank 2

_____   1. Unavoidably
_____   2. Only
_____   3. Troubled with uncertainty
_____   4. Reprimand; criticize
_____   5. Surrender under specified conditions
_____   6. Fervent; passionate
_____   7. Not clearly expressed; inexplicit
_____   8. Putting on a false appearance
_____   9. Cutting remarks
_____   10. Ability to act or speak without offending
_____   11. Kept secret to conceal an improper purpose
_____   12. Slight addition
_____   13. Difficult to bear; weighing heavily on the spirit
_____   14. Freed
_____   15. Jumble of loud noises
_____   16. Assailed
_____   17. Reserved; remote
_____   18. Stubborn
_____   19. Modest
_____   20. Provoked; full of resentment

Anne Frank Vocabulary Fill In The Blank 2 Answer Key

INEVITABLY	1. Unavoidably
SOLE	2. Only
PERPLEXED	3. Troubled with uncertainty
REBUKE	4. Reprimand; criticize
CAPITULATION	5. Surrender under specified conditions
ARDENT	6. Fervent; passionate
VAGUE	7. Not clearly expressed; inexplicit
SHAMMING	8. Putting on a false appearance
SARCASM	9. Cutting remarks
TACT	10. Ability to act or speak without offending
CLANDESTINE	11. Kept secret to conceal an improper purpose
TINGE	12. Slight addition
OPPRESSIVE	13. Difficult to bear; weighing heavily on the spirit
LIBERATED	14. Freed
DIN	15. Jumble of loud noises
PLIED	16. Assailed
ALOOF	17. Reserved; remote
OBSTINATE	18. Stubborn
UNASSUMING	19. Modest
PIQUED	20. Provoked; full of resentment

Anne Frank Vocabulary Fill In The Blank 3

_____ 1. Only

_____ 2. Characteristic of a woman who makes teasing romantic overtures

_____ 3. Improperly forward or bold

_____ 4. Provoked; full of resentment

_____ 5. Unavoidably

_____ 6. Offset; counterbalance; repayment

_____ 7. Reprimand; criticize

_____ 8. Difficult to bear; weighing heavily on the spirit

_____ 9. Putting on a false appearance

_____ 10. Friendly

_____ 11. To express sympathy

_____ 12. Stubborn

_____ 13. Cutting remarks

_____ 14. A fictitious name used by an author

_____ 15. Continually, without interruption

_____ 16. Not needed

_____ 17. Bother

_____ 18. Personal, movable property

_____ 19. Got by special effort; obtained

_____ 20. Adept; expert

Anne Frank Vocabulary Fill In The Blank 3 Answer Key

SOLE	1. Only
COQUETTISH	2. Characteristic of a woman who makes teasing romantic overtures
IMPERTINENT	3. Improperly forward or bold
PIQUED	4. Provoked; full of resentment
INEVITABLY	5. Unavoidably
COMPENSATION	6. Offset; counterbalance; repayment
REBUKE	7. Reprimand; criticize
OPPRESSIVE	8. Difficult to bear; weighing heavily on the spirit
SHAMMING	9. Putting on a false appearance
CONGENIAL	10. Friendly
CONDOLE	11. To express sympathy
OBSTINATE	12. Stubborn
SARCASM	13. Cutting remarks
PSEUDONYM	14. A fictitious name used by an author
INCESSANTLY	15. Continually, without interruption
SUPERFLUOUS	16. Not needed
NUISANCE	17. Bother
CHATTELS	18. Personal, movable property
PROCURED	19. Got by special effort; obtained
PROFICIENT	20. Adept; expert

Anne Frank Vocabulary Fill In The Blank 4

_____ 1. Difficult to bear; weighing heavily on the spirit

_____ 2. Despicable; contemptible

_____ 3. One who is excessively concerned with being proper

_____ 4. To become dull or boring

_____ 5. Modest

_____ 6. Troubled with uncertainty

_____ 7. Lack of basic necessities of life

_____ 8. Cutting remarks

_____ 9. Inclined to put up with beliefs, practices or traits of others

_____ 10. Ability to act or speak without offending

_____ 11. Not clearly expressed; inexplicit

_____ 12. A fictitious name used by an author

_____ 13. Characteristic of a woman who makes teasing romantic overtures

_____ 14. Skillful and adept under pressure

_____ 15. Assailed

_____ 16. Show plainly; reveal

_____ 17. Offset; counterbalance; repayment

_____ 18. Improperly forward or bold

_____ 19. Bother

_____ 20. Unavoidably

Anne Frank Vocabulary Fill In The Blank 4 Answer Key

OPPRESSIVE	1. Difficult to bear; weighing heavily on the spirit
DISDAINFUL	2. Despicable; contemptible
PRUDE	3. One who is excessively concerned with being proper
PALL	4. To become dull or boring
UNASSUMING	5. Modest
PERPLEXED	6. Troubled with uncertainty
PRIVATIONS	7. Lack of basic necessities of life
SARCASM	8. Cutting remarks
TOLERANT	9. Inclined to put up with beliefs, practices or traits of others
TACT	10. Ability to act or speak without offending
VAGUE	11. Not clearly expressed; inexplicit
PSEUDONYM	12. A fictitious name used by an author
COQUETTISH	13. Characteristic of a woman who makes teasing romantic overtures
ADROIT	14. Skillful and adept under pressure
PLIED	15. Assailed
MANIFEST	16. Show plainly; reveal
COMPENSATION	17. Offset; counterbalance; repayment
IMPERTINENT	18. Improperly forward or bold
NUISANCE	19. Bother
INEVITABLY	20. Unavoidably

Anne Frank Vocabulary Maching 1

___ 1. PLIED   A. Stubborn
___ 2. REBUKE   B. Cutting remarks
___ 3. INEVITABLY   C. Got by special effort; obtained
___ 4. CLANDESTINE   D. Person with an extreme enthusiasm for something
___ 5. CHATTELS   E. Mockingly
___ 6. FATALIST   F. Continually, without interruption
___ 7. PROCURED   G. Personal, movable property
___ 8. SHAMMING   H. Reserved; remote
___ 9. FANATIC   I. Offset; counterbalance; repayment
___10. ALOOF   J. Characterized by holding an unusually high opinion of oneself
___11. CONCEITED   K. One who believes all events are predetermined and inevitable
___12. CONGENIAL   L. Kept secret to conceal an improper purpose
___13. CAPITULATION   M. Fervent; passionate
___14. DISDAINFUL   N. Putting on a false appearance
___15. OBSTINATE   O. Surrender under specified conditions
___16. SCOFFINGLY   P. Assailed
___17. LIBERATED   Q. Reprimand; criticize
___18. COMPENSATION   R. Never to be forgotten
___19. ADROIT   S. Friendly
___20. ARDENT   T. Skillful and adept under pressure
___21. OPPRESSIVE   U. Unavoidably
___22. SARCASM   V. Freed
___23. IMMORTAL   W. Difficult to bear; weighing heavily on the spirit
___24. INCESSANTLY   X. Oddly
___25. QUEERLY   Y. Despicable; contemptible

Anne Frank Vocabulary Matching 1 Answer key

P - 1.	PLIED	A. Stubborn
Q - 2.	REBUKE	B. Cutting remarks
U - 3.	INEVITABLY	C. Got by special effort; obtained
L - 4.	CLANDESTINE	D. Person with an extreme enthusiasm for something
G - 5.	CHATTELS	E. Mockingly
K - 6.	FATALIST	F. Continually, without interruption
C - 7.	PROCURED	G. Personal, movable property
N - 8.	SHAMMING	H. Reserved; remote
D - 9.	FANATIC	I. Offset; counterbalance; repayment
H - 10.	ALOOF	J. Characterized by holding an unusually high opinion of oneself
J - 11.	CONCEITED	K. One who believes all events are predetermined and inevitable
S - 12.	CONGENIAL	L. Kept secret to conceal an improper purpose
O - 13.	CAPITULATION	M. Fervent; passionate
Y - 14.	DISDAINFUL	N. Putting on a false appearance
A - 15.	OBSTINATE	O. Surrender under specified conditions
E - 16.	SCOFFINGLY	P. Assailed
V - 17.	LIBERATED	Q. Reprimand; criticize
I - 18.	COMPENSATION	R. Never to be forgotten
T - 19.	ADROIT	S. Friendly
M - 20.	ARDENT	T. Skillful and adept under pressure
W - 21.	OPPRESSIVE	U. Unavoidably
B - 22.	SARCASM	V. Freed
R - 23.	IMMORTAL	W. Difficult to bear; weighing heavily on the spirit
F - 24.	INCESSANTLY	X. Oddly
X - 25.	QUEERLY	Y. Despicable; contemptible

Anne Frank Vocabulary Matching 2

___ 1. TACT
___ 2. LIBERATED
___ 3. ARDENT
___ 4. FANATIC
___ 5. PIQUED
___ 6. SOLE
___ 7. CAPITULATION
___ 8. SCOFFINGLY
___ 9. CONCEITED
___ 10. TOLERANT
___ 11. PSEUDONYM
___ 12. IMPERTINENT
___ 13. SUPERFLUOUS
___ 14. BLISS
___ 15. ADROIT
___ 16. FATUOUS
___ 17. DIN
___ 18. QUEERLY
___ 19. ADO
___ 20. DISDAINFUL
___ 21. ALOOF
___ 22. UNASSUMING
___ 23. LOATHE
___ 24. CONDOLE
___ 25. PRIVATIONS

A. Not needed
B. Only
C. Characterized by holding an unusually high opinion of oneself
D. Ability to act or speak without offending
E. Hate; extreme dislike
F. Mockingly
G. Foolish
H. Provoked; full of resentment
I. Lack of basic necessities of life
J. Inclined to put up with beliefs, practices or traits of others
K. Extreme happiness
L. Freed
M. Person with an extreme enthusiasm for something
N. Improperly forward or bold
O. Oddly
P. Fervent; passionate
Q. Despicable; contemptible
R. Jumble of loud noises
S. To express sympathy
T. Bustle; fuss; bother
U. Modest
V. A fictitious name used by an author
W. Skillful and adept under pressure
X. Surrender under specified conditions
Y. Reserved; remote

Anne Frank Vocabulary Matching 2 Answer Key

D - 1. TACT		A. Not needed
L - 2. LIBERATED		B. Only
P - 3. ARDENT		C. Characterized by holding an unusually high opinion of oneself
M - 4. FANATIC		D. Ability to act or speak without offending
H - 5. PIQUED		E. Hate; extreme dislike
B - 6. SOLE		F. Mockingly
X - 7. CAPITULATION		G. Foolish
F - 8. SCOFFINGLY		H. Provoked; full of resentment
C - 9. CONCEITED		I. Lack of basic necessities of life
J - 10. TOLERANT		J. Inclined to put up with beliefs, practices or traits of others
V - 11. PSEUDONYM		K. Extreme happiness
N - 12. IMPERTINENT		L. Freed
A - 13. SUPERFLUOUS		M. Person with an extreme enthusiasm for something
K - 14. BLISS		N. Improperly forward or bold
W - 15. ADROIT		O. Oddly
G - 16. FATUOUS		P. Fervent; passionate
R - 17. DIN		Q. Despicable; contemptible
O - 18. QUEERLY		R. Jumble of loud noises
T - 19. ADO		S. To express sympathy
Q - 20. DISDAINFUL		T. Bustle; fuss; bother
Y - 21. ALOOF		U. Modest
U - 22. UNASSUMING		V. A fictitious name used by an author
E - 23. LOATHE		W. Skillful and adept under pressure
S - 24. CONDOLE		X. Surrender under specified conditions
I - 25. PRIVATIONS		Y. Reserved; remote

Anne Frank Vocabulary Matching 3

___ 1. NUISANCE   A. Lack of basic necessities of life
___ 2. COMPENSATION   B. Characterized by holding an unusually high opinion of oneself
___ 3. TINGE   C. Oddly
___ 4. PRUDE   D. Bustle; fuss; bother
___ 5. FATALIST   E. Not needed
___ 6. CONCEITED   F. Bother
___ 7. LOATHE   G. One who believes all events are predetermined and inevitable
___ 8. DISDAINFUL   H. Skillful and adept under pressure
___ 9. CLANDESTINE   I. Adept; expert
___10. QUEERLY   J. Show plainly; reveal
___11. SARCASM   K. Offset; counterbalance; repayment
___12. ADO   L. One who is excessively concerned with being proper
___13. MANIFEST   M. Loud; lacking in restraint or discipline
___14. SUPERFLUOUS   N. Kept secret to conceal an improper purpose
___15. ADROIT   O. Cutting remarks
___16. IMMORTAL   P. Putting on a false appearance
___17. BOISTEROUS   Q. Improperly forward or bold
___18. PRIVATIONS   R. Never to be forgotten
___19. SCOFFINGLY   S. Slight addition
___20. CHATTELS   T. Characteristic of a woman who makes teasing romantic overtures
___21. COQUETTISH   U. Hate; extreme dislike
___22. PROFICIENT   V. Troubled with uncertainty
___23. SHAMMING   W. Despicable; contemptible
___24. PERPLEXED   X. Personal, movable property
___25. IMPERTINENT   Y. Mockingly

Anne Frank Vocabulary Matching 3 Answer Key

F - 1.	NUISANCE	A. Lack of basic necessities of life
K - 2.	COMPENSATION	B. Characterized by holding an unusually high opinion of oneself
S - 3.	TINGE	C. Oddly
L - 4.	PRUDE	D. Bustle; fuss; bother
G - 5.	FATALIST	E. Not needed
B - 6.	CONCEITED	F. Bother
U - 7.	LOATHE	G. One who believes all events are predetermined and inevitable
W - 8.	DISDAINFUL	H. Skillful and adept under pressure
N - 9.	CLANDESTINE	I. Adept; expert
C - 10.	QUEERLY	J. Show plainly; reveal
O - 11.	SARCASM	K. Offset; counterbalance; repayment
D - 12.	ADO	L. One who is excessively concerned with being proper
J - 13.	MANIFEST	M. Loud; lacking in restraint or discipline
E - 14.	SUPERFLUOUS	N. Kept secret to conceal an improper purpose
H - 15.	ADROIT	O. Cutting remarks
R - 16.	IMMORTAL	P. Putting on a false appearance
M - 17.	BOISTEROUS	Q. Improperly forward or bold
A - 18.	PRIVATIONS	R. Never to be forgotten
Y - 19.	SCOFFINGLY	S. Slight addition
X - 20.	CHATTELS	T. Characteristic of a woman who makes teasing romantic overtures
T - 21.	COQUETTISH	U. Hate; extreme dislike
I - 22.	PROFICIENT	V. Troubled with uncertainty
P - 23.	SHAMMING	W. Despicable; contemptible
V - 24.	PERPLEXED	X. Personal, movable property
Q - 25.	IMPERTINENT	Y. Mockingly

Anne Frank Vocabulary Matching 4

___ 1. LOATHE   A. Assailed
___ 2. MANIFEST   B. To become dull or boring
___ 3. IMMORTAL   C. Modest
___ 4. BLISS   D. Stubborn
___ 5. TOLERANT   E. Only
___ 6. UNASSUMING   F. Bother
___ 7. ADO   G. Continually, without interruption
___ 8. CAPITULATION   H. Despicable; contemptible
___ 9. PIQUED   I. To express sympathy
___ 10. OBSTINATE   J. Reprimand; criticize
___ 11. REBUKE   K. Show plainly; reveal
___ 12. TINGE   L. Inclined to put up with beliefs, practices or traits of others
___ 13. LIBERATED   M. Extreme happiness
___ 14. INCESSANTLY   N. Characterized by holding an unusually high opinion of oneself
___ 15. PLIED   O. One who is excessively concerned with being proper
___ 16. PRUDE   P. Slight addition
___ 17. CONCEITED   Q. Not clearly expressed; inexplicit
___ 18. CLANDESTINE   R. Surrender under specified conditions
___ 19. ADROIT   S. Kept secret to conceal an improper purpose
___ 20. CONDOLE   T. Provoked; full of resentment
___ 21. SOLE   U. Hate; extreme dislike
___ 22. DISDAINFUL   V. Bustle; fuss; bother
___ 23. PALL   W. Never to be forgotten
___ 24. VAGUE   X. Skillful and adept under pressure
___ 25. NUISANCE   Y. Freed

Anne Frank Vocabulary Matching 4 Answer Key

U - 1.	LOATHE	A. Assailed
K - 2.	MANIFEST	B. To become dull or boring
W - 3.	IMMORTAL	C. Modest
M - 4.	BLISS	D. Stubborn
L - 5.	TOLERANT	E. Only
C - 6.	UNASSUMING	F. Bother
V - 7.	ADO	G. Continually, without interruption
R - 8.	CAPITULATION	H. Despicable; contemptible
T - 9.	PIQUED	I. To express sympathy
D - 10.	OBSTINATE	J. Reprimand; criticize
J - 11.	REBUKE	K. Show plainly; reveal
P - 12.	TINGE	L. Inclined to put up with beliefs, practices or traits of others
Y - 13.	LIBERATED	M. Extreme happiness
G - 14.	INCESSANTLY	N. Characterized by holding an unusually high opinion of oneself
A - 15.	PLIED	O. One who is excessively concerned with being proper
O - 16.	PRUDE	P. Slight addition
N - 17.	CONCEITED	Q. Not clearly expressed; inexplicit
S - 18.	CLANDESTINE	R. Surrender under specified conditions
X - 19.	ADROIT	S. Kept secret to conceal an improper purpose
I - 20.	CONDOLE	T. Provoked; full of resentment
E - 21.	SOLE	U. Hate; extreme dislike
H - 22.	DISDAINFUL	V. Bustle; fuss; bother
B - 23.	PALL	W. Never to be forgotten
Q - 24.	VAGUE	X. Skillful and adept under pressure
F - 25.	NUISANCE	Y. Freed

Anne Frank Vocabulary Magic Squares 1

Match the definition with the vocabulary word. Put your answers in the magic squares below. When your answers are correct, all columns and rows will add to the same number.

A. PROCURED   E. IMMORTAL   I. PSEUDONYM   M. QUEERLY
B. OBSTINATE   F. VAGUE   J. OPPRESSIVE   N. PROFICIENT
C. FATALIST   G. BOISTEROUS K. TINGE   O. ALOOF
D. IMPERTINENT H. PIQUED   L. FATUOUS   P. DIN

1. Adept; expert
2. Loud; lacking in restraint or discipline
3. Foolish
4. Got by special effort; obtained
5. Slight addition
6. Stubborn
7. Oddly
8. Provoked; full of resentment
9. Never to be forgotten
10. Jumble of loud noises
11. One who believes all events are predetermined and inevitable
12. Difficult to bear; weighing heavily on the spirit
13. Improperly forward or bold
14. A fictitious name used by an author
15. Not clearly expressed; inexplicit
16. Reserved; remote

A=	B=	C=	D=
E=	F=	G=	H=
I=	J=	K=	L=
M=	N=	O=	P=

Anne Frank Vocabulary Magic Squares 1 Answer Key

Match the definition with the vocabulary word. Put your answers in the magic squares below. When your answers are correct, all columns and rows will add to the same number.

A. PROCURED
B. OBSTINATE
C. FATALIST
D. IMPERTINENT
E. IMMORTAL
F. VAGUE
G. BOISTEROUS
H. PIQUED
I. PSEUDONYM
J. OPPRESSIVE
K. TINGE
L. FATUOUS
M. QUEERLY
N. PROFICIENT
O. ALOOF
P. DIN

1. Adept; expert
2. Loud; lacking in restraint or discipline
3. Foolish
4. Got by special effort; obtained
5. Slight addition
6. Stubborn
7. Oddly
8. Provoked; full of resentment
9. Never to be forgotten
10. Jumble of loud noises
11. One who believes all events are predetermined and inevitable
12. Difficult to bear; weighing heavily on the spirit
13. Improperly forward or bold
14. A fictitious name used by an author
15. Not clearly expressed; inexplicit
16. Reserved; remote

A=4	B=6	C=11	D=13
E=9	F=15	G=2	H=8
I=14	J=12	K=5	L=3
M=7	N=1	O=16	P=10

Anne Frank Vocabulary Magic Squares 2

Match the definition with the vocabulary word. Put your answers in the magic squares below. When your answers are correct, all columns and rows will add to the same number.

A. ADO
B. PLIED
C. LIBERATED
D. CONDOLE
E. PERPLEXED
F. COMPENSATION
G. CHATTELS
H. DISDAINFUL
I. SARCASM
J. UNASSUMING
K. OPPRESSIVE
L. ADROIT
M. INCESSANTLY
N. SHAMMING
O. SCOFFINGLY
P. PSEUDONYM

1. Despicable; contemptible
2. Bustle; fuss; bother
3. Assailed
4. Personal, movable property
5. Modest
6. Mockingly
7. A fictitious name used by an author
8. Cutting remarks
9. Difficult to bear; weighing heavily on the spirit
10. Putting on a false appearance
11. Continually, without interruption
12. Skillful and adept under pressure
13. Troubled with uncertainty
14. To express sympathy
15. Freed
16. Offset; counterbalance; repayment

A=	B=	C=	D=
E=	F=	G=	H=
I=	J=	K=	L=
M=	N=	O=	P=

Anne Frank Vocabulary Magic Squares 2 Answer Key

Match the definition with the vocabulary word. Put your answers in the magic squares below. When your answers are correct, all columns and rows will add to the same number.

- A. ADO
- B. PLIED
- C. LIBERATED
- D. CONDOLE
- E. PERPLEXED
- F. COMPENSATION
- G. CHATTELS
- H. DISDAINFUL
- I. SARCASM
- J. UNASSUMING
- K. OPPRESSIVE
- L. ADROIT
- M. INCESSANTLY
- N. SHAMMING
- O. SCOFFINGLY
- P. PSEUDONYM

1. Despicable; contemptible
2. Bustle; fuss; bother
3. Assailed
4. Personal, movable property
5. Modest
6. Mockingly
7. A fictitious name used by an author
8. Cutting remarks
9. Difficult to bear; weighing heavily on the spirit
10. Putting on a false appearance
11. Continually, without interruption
12. Skillful and adept under pressure
13. Troubled with uncertainty
14. To express sympathy
15. Freed
16. Offset; counterbalance; repayment

A=2	B=3	C=15	D=14
E=13	F=16	G=4	H=1
I=8	J=5	K=9	L=12
M=11	N=10	O=6	P=7

Copyrighted

Anne Frank Vocabulary Magic Squares 3

Match the definition with the vocabulary word. Put your answers in the magic squares below. When your answers are correct, all columns and rows will add to the same number.

A. COMPENSATION
B. ADO
C. PROCURED
D. ADROIT
E. COQUETTISH
F. REBUKE
G. PERPLEXED
H. SCOFFINGLY
I. QUEERLY
J. FATUOUS
K. ALOOF
L. TINGE
M. UNASSUMING
N. SOLE
O. ARDENT
P. OBSTINATE

1. Bustle; fuss; bother
2. Troubled with uncertainty
3. Reserved; remote
4. Only
5. Modest
6. Slight addition
7. Mockingly
8. Offset; counterbalance; repayment
9. Stubborn
10. Oddly
11. Characteristic of a woman who makes teasing romantic overtures
12. Skillful and adept under pressure
13. Got by special effort; obtained
14. Reprimand; criticize
15. Foolish
16. Fervent; passionate

A=	B=	C=	D=
E=	F=	G=	H=
I=	J=	K=	L=
M=	N=	O=	P=

Anne Frank Vocabulary Magic Squares 3 Answer Key

Match the definition with the vocabulary word. Put your answers in the magic squares below. When your answers are correct, all columns and rows will add to the same number.

A. COMPENSATION   E. COQUETTISH   I. QUEERLY   M. UNASSUMING
B. ADO   F. REBUKE   J. FATUOUS   N. SOLE
C. PROCURED   G. PERPLEXED   K. ALOOF   O. ARDENT
D. ADROIT   H. SCOFFINGLY   L. TINGE   P. OBSTINATE

1. Bustle; fuss; bother
2. Troubled with uncertainty
3. Reserved; remote
4. Only
5. Modest
6. Slight addition
7. Mockingly
8. Offset; counterbalance; repayment
9. Stubborn
10. Oddly
11. Characteristic of a woman who makes teasing romantic overtures
12. Skillful and adept under pressure
13. Got by special effort; obtained
14. Reprimand; criticize
15. Foolish
16. Fervent; passionate

A=8	B=1	C=13	D=12
E=11	F=14	G=2	H=7
I=10	J=15	K=3	L=6
M=5	N=4	O=16	P=9

Anne Frank Vocabulary Magic Squares 4

Match the definition with the vocabulary word. Put your answers in the magic squares below. When your answers are correct, all columns and rows will add to the same number.

A. MANIFEST
B. SHAMMING
C. ALOOF
D. LOATHE
E. CONGENIAL
F. PROFICIENT
G. UNASSUMING
H. REBUKE
I. SUPERFLUOUS
J. TINGE
K. IMPERTINENT
L. CAPITULATION
M. CONCEITED
N. FATALIST
O. SARCASM
P. FATUOUS

1. Reserved; remote
2. Slight addition
3. Adept; expert
4. Cutting remarks
5. Foolish
6. Friendly
7. Not needed
8. Hate; extreme dislike
9. Characterized by holding an unusually high opinion of oneself
10. Reprimand; criticize
11. Surrender under specified conditions
12. Show plainly; reveal
13. Putting on a false appearance
14. Improperly forward or bold
15. Modest
16. One who believes all events are predetermined and inevitable

A=	B=	C=	D=
E=	F=	G=	H=
I=	J=	K=	L=
M=	N=	O=	P=

Anne Frank Vocabulary Magic Squares 4 Answer Key

Match the definition with the vocabulary word. Put your answers in the magic squares below. When your answers are correct, all columns and rows will add to the same number.

A. MANIFEST
B. SHAMMING
C. ALOOF
D. LOATHE
E. CONGENIAL
F. PROFICIENT
G. UNASSUMING
H. REBUKE
I. SUPERFLUOUS
J. TINGE
K. IMPERTINENT
L. CAPITULATION
M. CONCEITED
N. FATALIST
O. SARCASM
P. FATUOUS

1. Reserved; remote
2. Slight addition
3. Adept; expert
4. Cutting remarks
5. Foolish
6. Friendly
7. Not needed
8. Hate; extreme dislike
9. Characterized by holding an unusually high opinion of oneself
10. Reprimand; criticize
11. Surrender under specified conditions
12. Show plainly; reveal
13. Putting on a false appearance
14. Improperly forward or bold
15. Modest
16. One who believes all events are predetermined and inevitable

A=12	B=13	C=1	D=8
E=6	F=3	G=15	H=10
I=7	J=2	K=14	L=11
M=9	N=16	O=4	P=5

Anne Frank Vocabulary Word Search 1

```
S H A M M I N G P R I V A T I O N S B S
N O I T A S N E P M O C R D L L W H V Y
M T C L A N D E S T I N E E R O R S X D
Q L D G S Z H B V O M C G E B O A I L K
R S Q S V A J W R I L N P G V U I T Z M
H N U G W P R H C W T E U N H A K T H K
P K M P T V L C R O P A Q I F N G E N E
Y T T G E D T X A F N I B T S P R U D E
L T O L E R A N T S M G Q L L A P Q E B
T N E I C I F O R P M X E U Y F N O L Q
N M G G F M P L E S E P F N E T A C T G
A A K H R A V R U P R R Z A I D H L E K
S N S U O U T A F O P M P D N A L O O F
S I H B T I C A C H U S W L T A L P K L
E F H Z N V X U L Z S S Y T E C T L T W
C E D E T A R E B I L Y E F A X D I N L
N S N Q U E E R L Y S L C G D M E E C R
I T N E D R A B O I S T E R O U S D M R
```

Ability to act or speak without offending (4)
Adept; expert (10)
Assailed (5)
Bother (8)
Bustle; fuss; bother (3)
Characteristic of a woman who makes teasing romantic overtures (10)
Continually, without interruption (11)
Cutting remarks (7)
Extreme happiness (5)
Fervent; passionate (6)
Foolish (7)
Freed (9)
Friendly (9)
Got by special effort; obtained (8)
Hate; extreme dislike (6)
Improperly forward or bold (11)
Inclined to put up with beliefs, practices or traits of others (8)
Jumble of loud noises (3)
Kept secret to conceal an improper purpose (11)
Lack of basic necessities of life (10)
Loud; lacking in restraint or discipline (10)
Not clearly expressed; inexplicit (5)
Not needed (11)
Oddly (7)
Offset; counterbalance; repayment (12)

One who believes all events are predetermined and inevitable (8)
One who is excessively concerned with being proper (5)
Only (4)
Person with an extreme enthusiasm for something (7)
Personal, movable property (8)
Provoked; full of resentment (6)
Putting on a false appearance (8)
Reprimand; criticize (6)
Reserved; remote (5)
Show plainly; reveal (8)
Skillful and adept under pressure (6)
Slight addition (5)
To become dull or boring (4)
Troubled with uncertainty (9)
Unavoidably (10)

Anne Frank Vocabulary Word Search 1 Answer Key

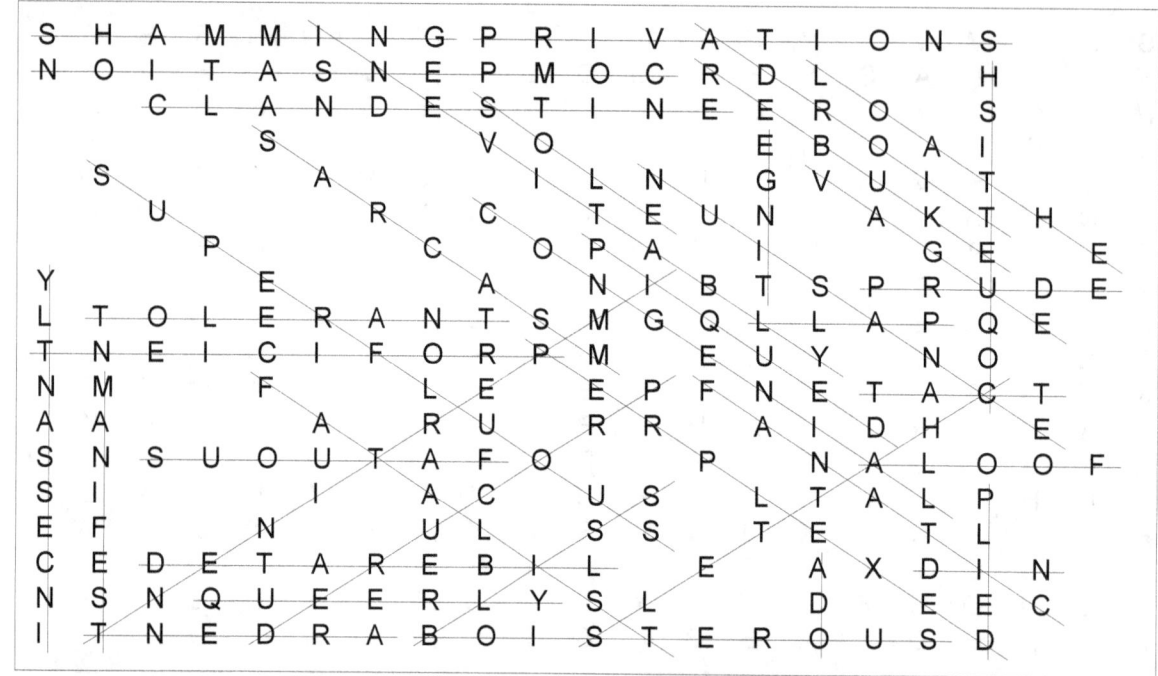

Ability to act or speak without offending (4)
Adept; expert (10)
Assailed (5)
Bother (8)
Bustle; fuss; bother (3)
Characteristic of a woman who makes teasing romantic overtures (10)
Continually, without interruption (11)
Cutting remarks (7)
Extreme happiness (5)
Fervent; passionate (6)
Foolish (7)
Freed (9)
Friendly (9)
Got by special effort; obtained (8)
Hate; extreme dislike (6)
Improperly forward or bold (11)
Inclined to put up with beliefs, practices or traits of others (8)
Jumble of loud noises (3)
Kept secret to conceal an improper purpose (11)
Lack of basic necessities of life (10)
Loud; lacking in restraint or discipline (10)
Not clearly expressed; inexplicit (5)
Not needed (11)
Oddly (7)
Offset; counterbalance; repayment (12)

One who believes all events are predetermined and inevitable (8)
One who is excessively concerned with being proper (5)
Only (4)
Person with an extreme enthusiasm for something (7)
Personal, movable property (8)
Provoked; full of resentment (6)
Putting on a false appearance (8)
Reprimand; criticize (6)
Reserved; remote (5)
Show plainly; reveal (8)
Skillful and adept under pressure (6)
Slight addition (5)
To become dull or boring (4)
Troubled with uncertainty (9)
Unavoidably (10)

Anne Frank Vocabulary Word Search 2

```
S C O F F I N G L Y A D O L A R D E N T
R P R O C U R E D E V M A O S N I W V S
P Y O C O T X D C C J D X A U D N Z L J
G L F A N D F N N T R P X T O X X E P V
A Y J P C M A T D O B A Q H U R T S T P
F L Z I E S M H I R R L E E T T F D S H
O B S T I N A T E T O L E R A N T G I Z
S A D U T M Y N O T O B H H F M N T L K
A T N L E J M G P S S L C S P I X W A K
R I F A D X Z O P V K I W R M D D W T L
C V A T J L D R R G B S T M E E U G A V
A E N I G E U E E T Y S A X T G E I F Q
S N A O G D Q B S P A H E A G L N T C H
M I T N E J C U S R S L R Z O E G N W M
P L I E D Y D K I Z P E P D G T A C T Z
S T C Z N C H E V R B H N N Y T Q P X K
M A N I F E S T E I W O O P H Y Z R W B
Q U E E R L Y P L V C C P I Q U E D Q V
```

Ability to act or speak without offending (4)
Assailed (5)
Bother (8)
Bustle; fuss; bother (3)
Characterized by holding an unusually high opinion of oneself (9)
Cutting remarks (7)
Difficult to bear; weighing heavily on the spirit (10)
Extreme happiness (5)
Fervent; passionate (6)
Foolish (7)
Freed (9)
Friendly (9)
Got by special effort; obtained (8)
Hate; extreme dislike (6)
Inclined to put up with beliefs, practices or traits of others (8)
Jumble of loud noises (3)
Mockingly (10)
Never to be forgotten (8)
Not clearly expressed; inexplicit (5)
Oddly (7)
One who believes all events are predetermined and inevitable (8)
One who is excessively concerned with being proper (5)
Only (4)
Person with an extreme enthusiasm for something (7)
Personal, movable property (8)
Provoked; full of resentment (6)
Putting on a false appearance (8)
Reprimand; criticize (6)
Reserved; remote (5)
Show plainly; reveal (8)
Skillful and adept under pressure (6)
Slight addition (5)
Stubborn (9)
Surrender under specified conditions (12)
To become dull or boring (4)
To express sympathy (7)
Troubled with uncertainty (9)
Unavoidably (10)

Anne Frank Vocabulary Word Search 2 Answer Key

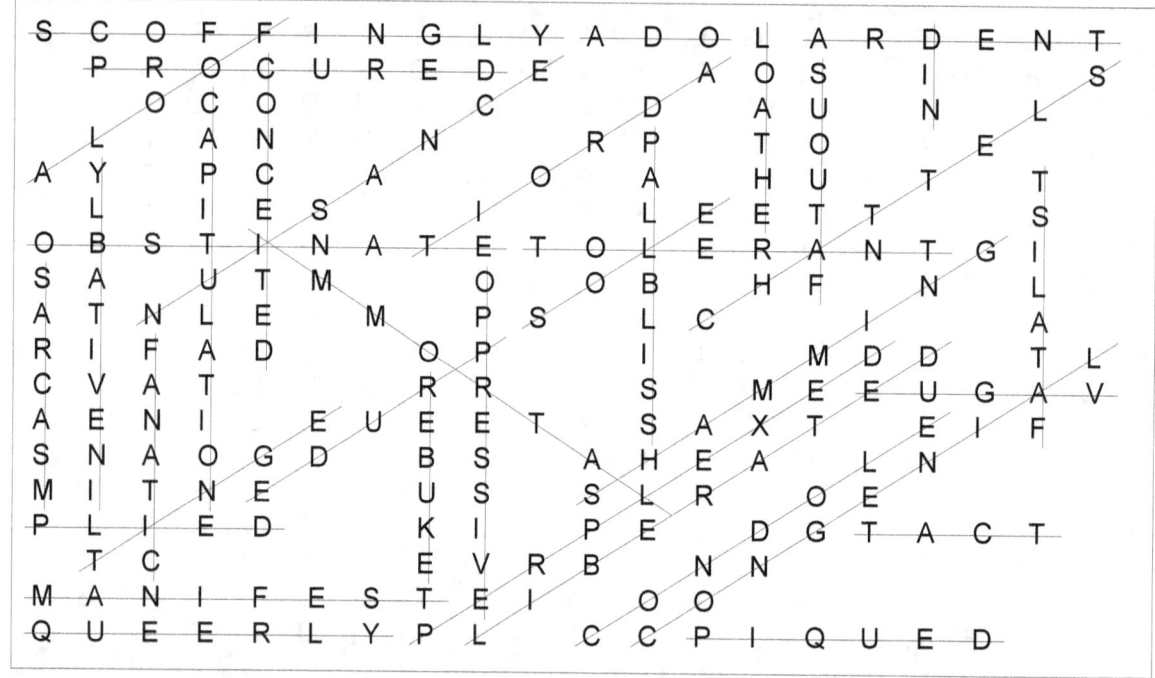

Ability to act or speak without offending (4)
Assailed (5)
Bother (8)
Bustle; fuss; bother (3)
Characterized by holding an unusually high opinion of oneself (9)
Cutting remarks (7)
Difficult to bear; weighing heavily on the spirit (10)
Extreme happiness (5)
Fervent; passionate (6)
Foolish (7)
Freed (9)
Friendly (9)
Got by special effort; obtained (8)
Hate; extreme dislike (6)
Inclined to put up with beliefs, practices or traits of others (8)
Jumble of loud noises (3)
Mockingly (10)
Never to be forgotten (8)
Not clearly expressed; inexplicit (5)
Oddly (7)
One who believes all events are predetermined and inevitable (8)
One who is excessively concerned with being proper (5)
Only (4)

Person with an extreme enthusiasm for something (7)
Personal, movable property (8)
Provoked; full of resentment (6)
Putting on a false appearance (8)
Reprimand; criticize (6)
Reserved; remote (5)
Show plainly; reveal (8)
Skillful and adept under pressure (6)
Slight addition (5)
Stubborn (9)
Surrender under specified conditions (12)
To become dull or boring (4)
To express sympathy (7)
Troubled with uncertainty (9)
Unavoidably (10)

Anne Frank Vocabulary Word Search 3

```
T S I L A T A F S P C F Q H A J S R Z X
S C A P I T U L A T I O N W M R E O C Q
N D V R I M E P N N B O N M Y G D J L W
O F I O C T A E I S X L N D N A U E A E
I I R S T A I N T Q N A E I O Y R P N F
T D N A D C S I I U V T P D L P L D T
A S H E I A N M D F I E N E U R E I E Q
V C C F V A I S T S E T D R E E P E S P
I S O O T I E N S A S S O P S E A D T H
R R H E F U T E F S C F T L P U L D I G
P L P A G F R A I U E T I E E Q L W N M
F Z O A M P I L B C L G M X G R V Q E M
A D V A P M B N N L F F M E J S A K F F
T X D O T S I A G C Y R O D T S U N B J
U B Q S K H S N T L S J R G J B H X T T
O Z T Q R I E W G T Y Z T K E F H W D V
U C O Q U E T T I S H T A R M P L J T V
S S S N D E T A R E B I L F A N A T I C
```

ADO	COQUETTISH	LOATHE	PRIVATIONS	SOLE
ADROIT	DIN	MANIFEST	PROFICIENT	TACT
ALOOF	DISDAINFUL	NUISANCE	PRUDE	TINGE
ARDENT	FANATIC	OBSTINATE	PSEUDONYM	TOLERANT
BLISS	FATALIST	OPPRESSIVE	QUEERLY	VAGUE
CAPITULATION	FATUOUS	PALL	REBUKE	
CHATTELS	IMMORTAL	PERPLEXED	SARCASM	
CLANDESTINE	INEVITABLY	PIQUED	SCOFFINGLY	
CONDOLE	LIBERATED	PLIED	SHAMMING	

Anne Frank Vocabulary Word Search 3 Answer Key

ADO	COQUETTISH	LOATHE	PRIVATIONS	SOLE
ADROIT	DIN	MANIFEST	PROFICIENT	TACT
ALOOF	DISDAINFUL	NUISANCE	PRUDE	TINGE
ARDENT	FANATIC	OBSTINATE	PSEUDONYM	TOLERANT
BLISS	FATALIST	OPPRESSIVE	QUEERLY	VAGUE
CAPITULATION	FATUOUS	PALL	REBUKE	
CHATTELS	IMMORTAL	PERPLEXED	SARCASM	
CLANDESTINE	INEVITABLY	PIQUED	SCOFFINGLY	
CONDOLE	LIBERATED	PLIED	SHAMMING	

Anne Frank Vocabulary Word Search 4

```
O B V Z P W S U O L F R E P U S B S B
P E R P L E X E D B X C O N G E N I A L
P Y G Y C D U N A S S U M I N G S E R B
R L P R O C U R E D P T B L I M Q L C H
E R I H N V K T C N A A I N M W T O A X
S E W B C I M W N Z L L N N M C Z D S R
S Z Z S E T N A R E L O T L A D O N M C
I U C L I R K E P F I O U T H T O O D W
V Q O N T R A S V T A F A S S I E C N Z
E S A D E M E T A I N N N T T G E I U C
U P R L D U A L E I T O A A H D D M I Z
G Y D K D T U N A D I A S T U E S M S F
A Q E O A T I D I T B N B R I U R O A Z
V X N T I D S N A F E L P L O C E R N S
X Y T P E I R V G P E D I U Y C B T C S
M Z A I D G I O M E G S T S B L U A E H
G C L M W R L O I G C A T H S H K L X L
Z P M P P Y C N H T F P P I Q U E D L Y
```

ADO	DISDAINFUL	PALL	SHAMMING
ADROIT	FANATIC	PERPLEXED	SOLE
ALOOF	FATUOUS	PIQUED	SUPERFLUOUS
ARDENT	IMMORTAL	PLIED	TACT
BLISS	INEVITABLY	PRIVATIONS	TINGE
CAPITULATION	LIBERATED	PROCURED	TOLERANT
COMPENSATION	LOATHE	PRUDE	UNASSUMING
CONCEITED	MANIFEST	PSEUDONYM	VAGUE
CONDOLE	NUISANCE	QUEERLY	
CONGENIAL	OBSTINATE	REBUKE	
DIN	OPPRESSIVE	SARCASM	

Anne Frank Vocabulary Word Search 4 Answer Key

ADO	DISDAINFUL	PALL	SHAMMING
ADROIT	FANATIC	PERPLEXED	SOLE
ALOOF	FATUOUS	PIQUED	SUPERFLUOUS
ARDENT	IMMORTAL	PLIED	TACT
BLISS	INEVITABLY	PRIVATIONS	TINGE
CAPITULATION	LIBERATED	PROCURED	TOLERANT
COMPENSATION	LOATHE	PRUDE	UNASSUMING
CONCEITED	MANIFEST	PSEUDONYM	VAGUE
CONDOLE	NUISANCE	QUEERLY	
CONGENIAL	OBSTINATE	REBUKE	
DIN	OPPRESSIVE	SARCASM	

Anne Frank Vocabulary Crossword 1

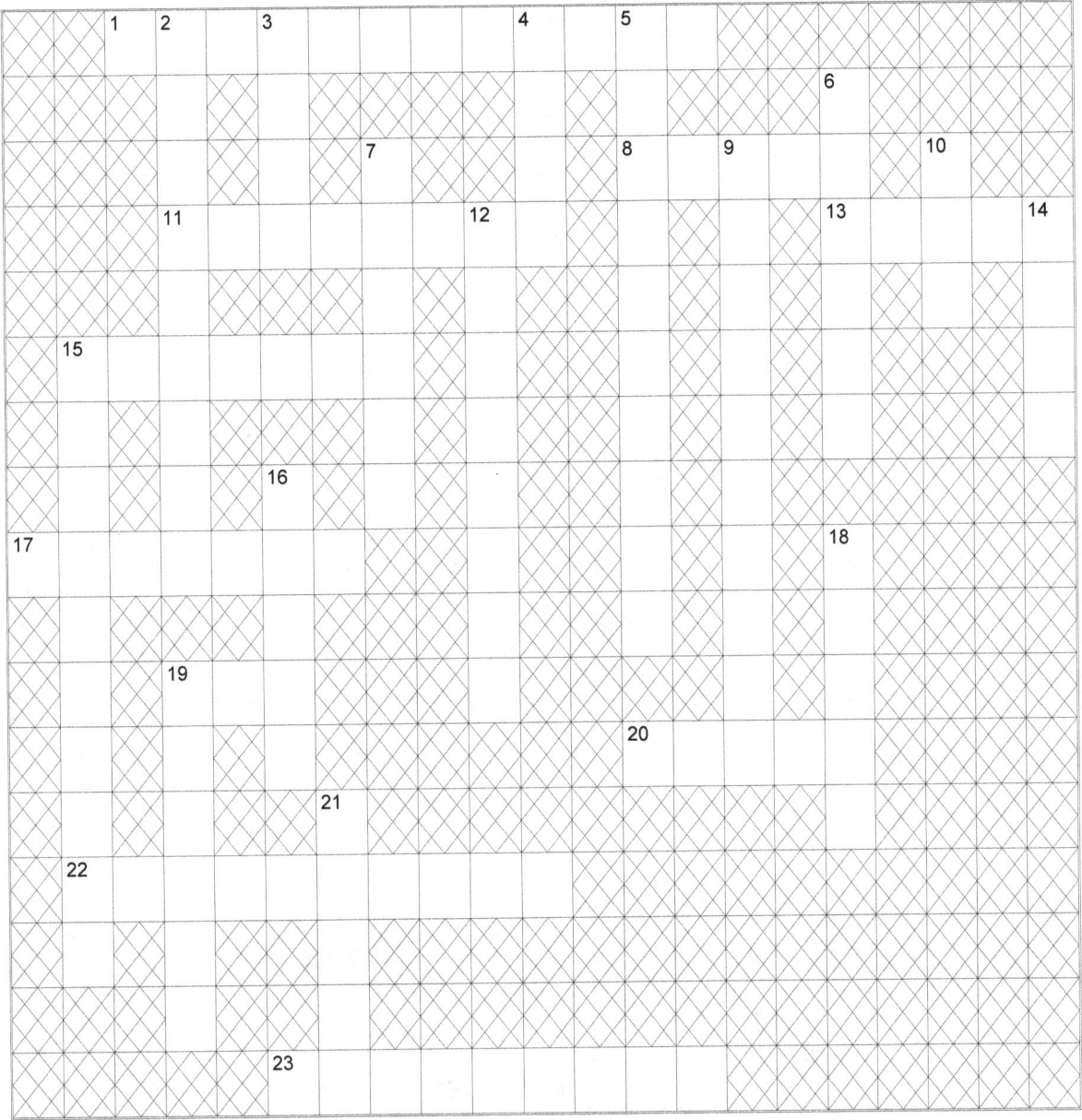

Across
1. Offset; counterbalance; repayment
8. One who is excessively concerned with being proper
11. Inclined to put up with beliefs, practices or traits of others
13. Extreme happiness
15. To express sympathy
17. Oddly
19. Bustle; fuss; bother
20. Not clearly expressed; inexplicit
22. Mockingly
23. Troubled with uncertainty

Down
2. Stubborn
3. To become dull or boring
4. Ability to act or speak without offending
5. Difficult to bear; weighing heavily on the spirit
6. Reprimand; criticize
7. Fervent; passionate
9. Modest
10. Jumble of loud noises
12. Bother
14. Only
15. Characteristic of a woman who makes teasing romantic overtures
16. Reserved; remote
18. Assailed
19. Skillful and adept under pressure
21. Slight addition

Anne Frank Vocabulary Crossword 1 Answer Key

Across
1. Offset; counterbalance; repayment
8. One who is excessively concerned with being proper
11. Inclined to put up with beliefs, practices or traits of others
13. Extreme happiness
15. To express sympathy
17. Oddly
19. Bustle; fuss; bother
20. Not clearly expressed; inexplicit
22. Mockingly
23. Troubled with uncertainty

Down
2. Stubborn
3. To become dull or boring
4. Ability to act or speak without offending
5. Difficult to bear; weighing heavily on the spirit
6. Reprimand; criticize
7. Fervent; passionate
9. Modest
10. Jumble of loud noises
12. Bother
14. Only
15. Characteristic of a woman who makes teasing romantic overtures
16. Reserved; remote
18. Assailed
19. Skillful and adept under pressure
21. Slight addition

Anne Frank Vocabulary Crossword 2

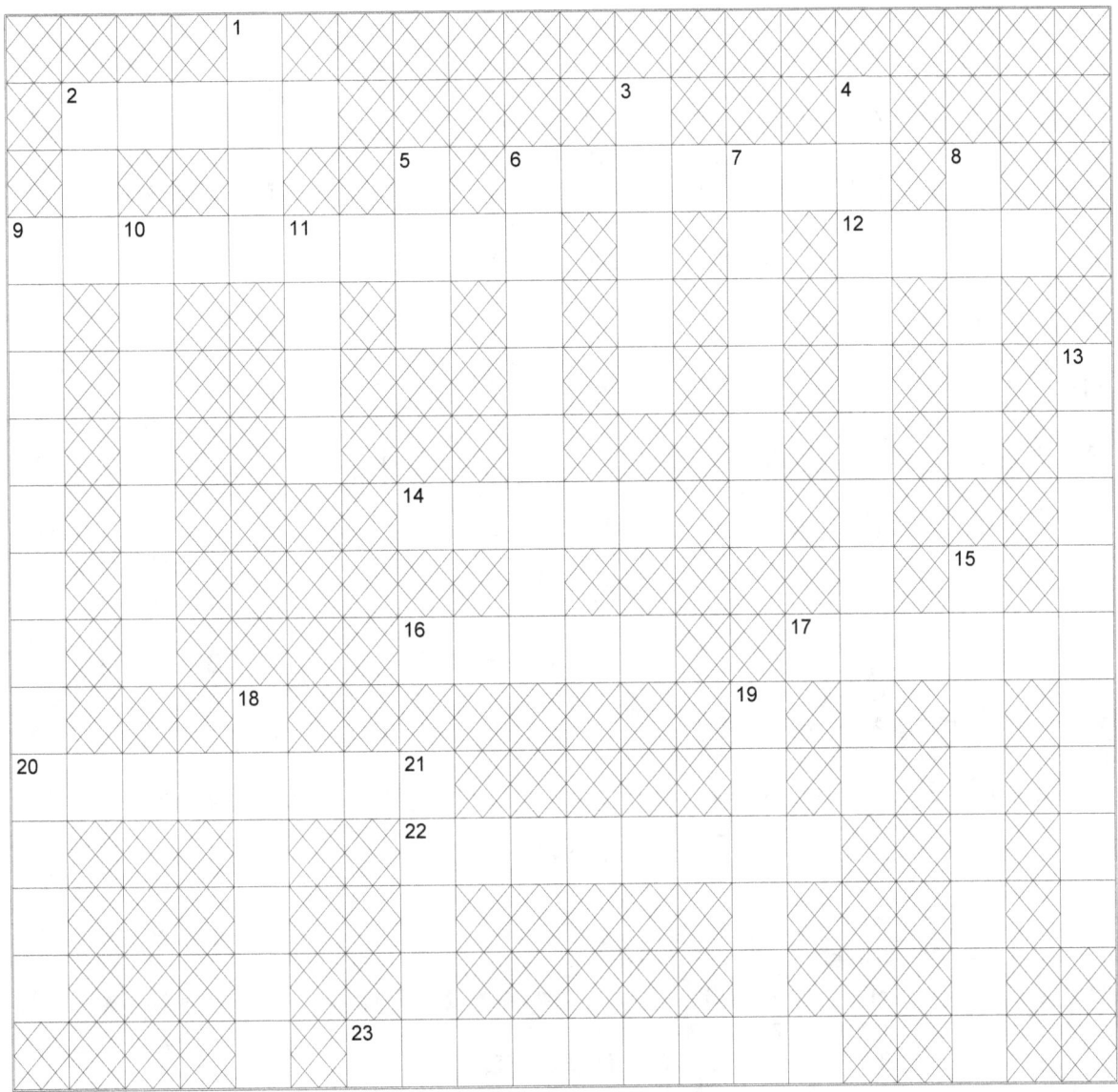

Across
2. Reserved; remote
6. Cutting remarks
9. Characteristic of a woman who makes teasing romantic overtures
12. To become dull or boring
14. Assailed
16. Not clearly expressed; inexplicit
17. Reprimand; criticize
20. Inclined to put up with beliefs, practices or traits of others
22. Never to be forgotten
23. Troubled with uncertainty

Down
1. Only
2. Bustle; fuss; bother
3. One who is excessively concerned with being proper
4. Improperly forward or bold
5. Jumble of loud noises
6. Putting on a false appearance
7. Skillful and adept under pressure
8. Extreme happiness
9. Offset; counterbalance; repayment
10. Oddly
11. Ability to act or speak without offending
13. Characterized by holding an unusually high opinion of oneself
15. Bother
18. Fervent; passionate
19. Hate; extreme dislike
21. Slight addition

Anne Frank Vocabulary Crossword 2 Answer Key

Across
- 2. Reserved; remote
- 6. Cutting remarks
- 9. Characteristic of a woman who makes teasing romantic overtures
- 12. To become dull or boring
- 14. Assailed
- 16. Not clearly expressed; inexplicit
- 17. Reprimand; criticize
- 20. Inclined to put up with beliefs, practices or traits of others
- 22. Never to be forgotten
- 23. Troubled with uncertainty

Down
- 1. Only
- 2. Bustle; fuss; bother
- 3. One who is excessively concerned with being proper
- 4. Improperly forward or bold
- 5. Jumble of loud noises
- 6. Putting on a false appearance
- 7. Skillful and adept under pressure
- 8. Extreme happiness
- 9. Offset; counterbalance; repayment
- 10. Oddly
- 11. Ability to act or speak without offending
- 13. Characterized by holding an unusually high opinion of oneself
- 15. Bother
- 18. Fervent; passionate
- 19. Hate; extreme dislike
- 21. Slight addition

Anne Frank Vocabulary Crossword 3

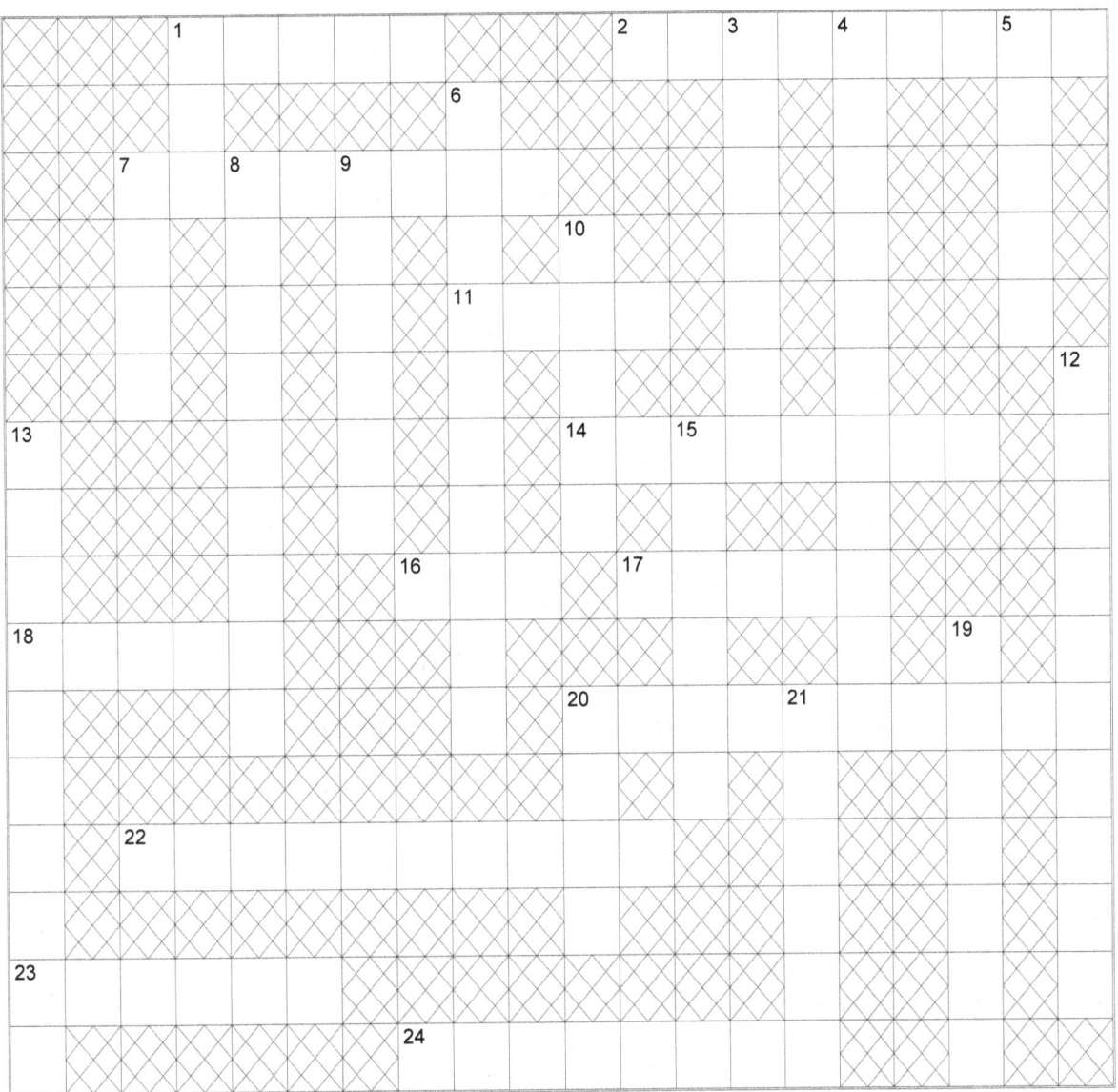

Across
1. Reserved; remote
2. Stubborn
7. Inclined to put up with beliefs, practices or traits of others
11. Only
14. Putting on a false appearance
16. Jumble of loud noises
17. One who is excessively concerned with being proper
18. Not clearly expressed; inexplicit
20. Lack of basic necessities of life
22. Mockingly
23. Hate; extreme dislike
24. One who believes all events are predetermined and inevitable

Down
1. Bustle; fuss; bother
3. Cutting remarks
4. Improperly forward or bold
5. Slight addition
6. Modest
7. Ability to act or speak without offending
8. Freed
9. Reprimand; criticize
10. Extreme happiness
12. Difficult to bear; weighing heavily on the spirit
13. Unavoidably
15. Skillful and adept under pressure
19. To express sympathy
20. To become dull or boring
21. Fervent; passionate

Anne Frank Vocabulary Crossword 3 Answer Key

Across
1. Reserved; remote
2. Stubborn
7. Inclined to put up with beliefs, practices or traits of others
11. Only
14. Putting on a false appearance
16. Jumble of loud noises
17. One who is excessively concerned with being proper
18. Not clearly expressed; inexplicit
20. Lack of basic necessities of life
22. Mockingly
23. Hate; extreme dislike
24. One who believes all events are predetermined and inevitable

Down
1. Bustle; fuss; bother
3. Cutting remarks
4. Improperly forward or bold
5. Slight addition
6. Modest
7. Ability to act or speak without offending
8. Freed
9. Reprimand; criticize
10. Extreme happiness
12. Difficult to bear; weighing heavily on the spirit
13. Unavoidably
15. Skillful and adept under pressure
19. To express sympathy
20. To become dull or boring
21. Fervent; passionate

Anne Frank Vocabulary Crossword 4

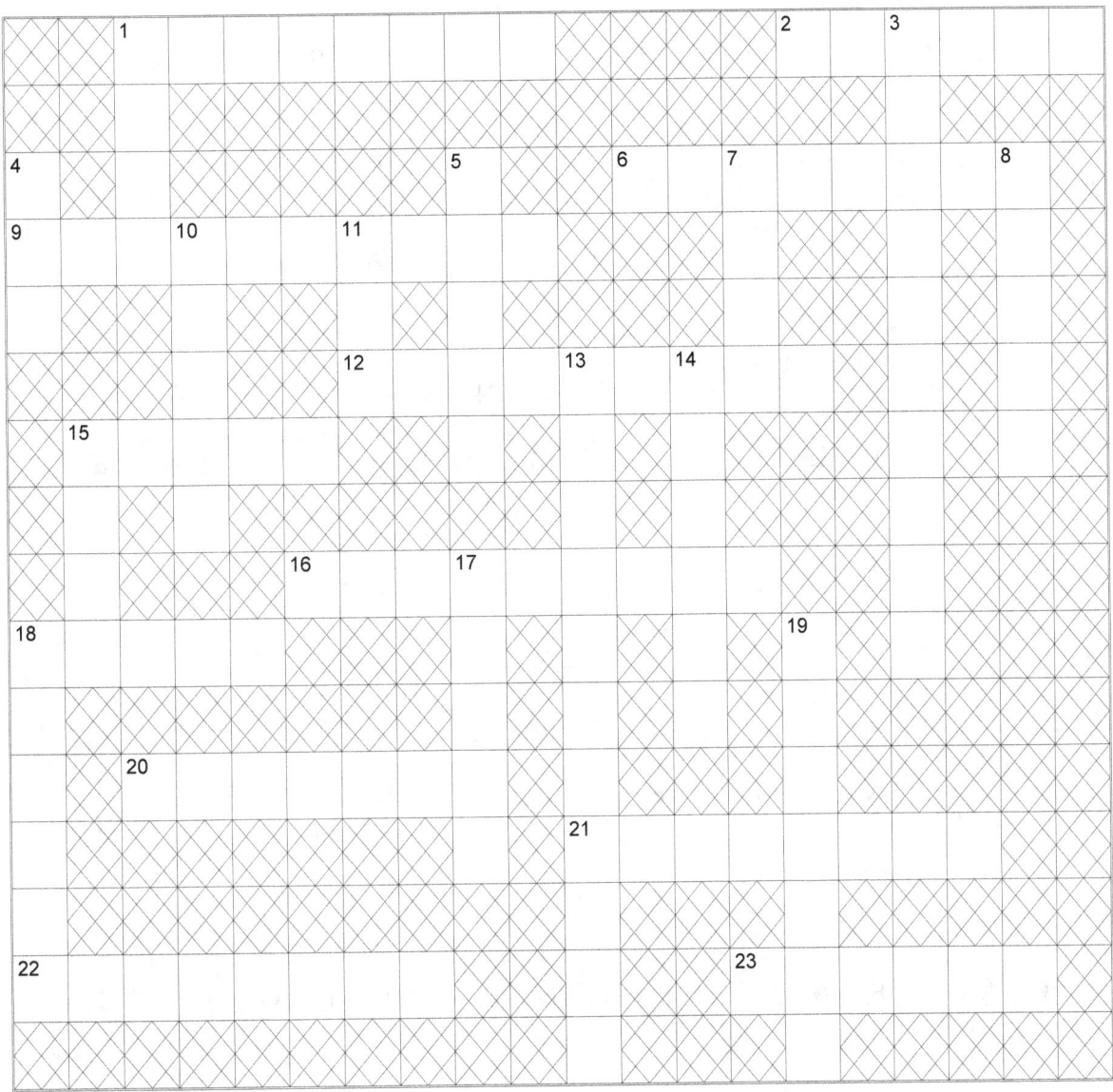

Across
1. Putting on a false appearance
2. Reprimand; criticize
6. One who believes all events are predetermined and inevitable
9. Unavoidably
12. Stubborn
15. One who is excessively concerned with being proper
16. Troubled with uncertainty
18. Reserved; remote
20. To express sympathy
21. Bother
22. Inclined to put up with beliefs, practices or traits of others
23. Provoked; full of resentment

Down
1. Only
3. Loud; lacking in restraint or discipline
4. Jumble of loud noises
5. Extreme happiness
7. Ability to act or speak without offending
8. Slight addition
10. Not clearly expressed; inexplicit
11. Bustle; fuss; bother
13. Improperly forward or bold
14. Fervent; passionate
15. To become dull or boring
17. Assailed
18. Skillful and adept under pressure
19. Person with an extreme enthusiasm for something

Anne Frank Vocabulary Crossword 4 Answer Key

```
        1                                         2   3
        S  H  A  M  M  I  N  G              R   E   B   U   K   E
        O                                            O
4                    5           6   7                   8
D       L            B           F   A   T   A   L   I   S   T
9          10           11
I   N   E   V   I   T   A   B   L   Y       A           S       I
N          A            D               I               C       N
                                                                G
           G            12          13   14
                        O   B   S   T   I   N   A   T   E       G
        15
        P   R   U   D   E               S       M       R       E
        A           E                       P       D       O
                        16          17
                        P   E   R   P   L   E   X   E   D       U
18
A   L   O   O   F           L           R       N       19
                                                        F       S
D                           I           T       T       A
        20
R       C   O   N   D   O   L   E       I               N
                                    21
O                           D           N   U   I   S   A   N   C   E
I                                       E               T
22                                                  23
T   O   L   E   R   A   N   T       N       P   I   Q   U   E   D
                                    T           C
```

Across
1. Putting on a false appearance
2. Reprimand; criticize
6. One who believes all events are predetermined and inevitable
9. Unavoidably
12. Stubborn
15. One who is excessively concerned with being proper
16. Troubled with uncertainty
18. Reserved; remote
20. To express sympathy
21. Bother
22. Inclined to put up with beliefs, practices or traits of others
23. Provoked; full of resentment

Down
1. Only
3. Loud; lacking in restraint or discipline
4. Jumble of loud noises
5. Extreme happiness
7. Ability to act or speak without offending
8. Slight addition
10. Not clearly expressed; inexplicit
11. Bustle; fuss; bother
13. Improperly forward or bold
14. Fervent; passionate
15. To become dull or boring
17. Assailed
18. Skillful and adept under pressure
19. Person with an extreme enthusiasm for something

Anne Frank Vocabulary Juggle Letters 1

1. OITMLRAM = 1. _____
Never to be forgotten

2. CAAITFN = 2. _____
Person with an extreme enthusiasm for something

3. EUREBK = 3. _____
Reprimand; criticize

4. PIOESEVPRS = 4. _____
Difficult to bear; weighing heavily on the spirit

5. CATT = 5. _____
Ability to act or speak without offending

6. VNPOTAIRSI = 6. _____
Lack of basic necessities of life

7. FSEMNITA = 7. _____
Show plainly; reveal

8. TUNIILTPCAOA = 8. _____
Surrender under specified conditions

9. CFFNYGOISL = 9. _____
Mockingly

10. NSTLIEYNSAC =10. _____
Continually, without interruption

11. DRNEAT =11. _____
Fervent; passionate

12. ISLBS =12. _____
Extreme happiness

13. ENCOANGLI =13. _____
Friendly

14. ALLP =14. _____
To become dull or boring

15. YTNILIEBAV =15. _____
Unavoidably

Anne Frank Vocabulary Juggle Letters 1 Answer Key

1. OITMLRAM = 1. IMMORTAL
   Never to be forgotten

2. CAAITFN = 2. FANATIC
   Person with an extreme enthusiasm for something

3. EUREBK = 3. REBUKE
   Reprimand; criticize

4. PIOESEVPRS = 4. OPPRESSIVE
   Difficult to bear; weighing heavily on the spirit

5. CATT = 5. TACT
   Ability to act or speak without offending

6. VNPOTAIRSI = 6. PRIVATIONS
   Lack of basic necessities of life

7. FSEMNITA = 7. MANIFEST
   Show plainly; reveal

8. TUNIILTPCAOA = 8. CAPITULATION
   Surrender under specified conditions

9. CFFNYGOISL = 9. SCOFFINGLY
   Mockingly

10. NSTLIEYNSAC = 10. INCESSANTLY
    Continually, without interruption

11. DRNEAT = 11. ARDENT
    Fervent; passionate

12. ISLBS = 12. BLISS
    Extreme happiness

13. ENCOANGLI = 13. CONGENIAL
    Friendly

14. ALLP = 14. PALL
    To become dull or boring

15. YTNILIEBAV = 15. INEVITABLY
    Unavoidably

Anne Frank Vocabulary Juggle Letters 2

1. AHETLO = 1. _____
   Hate; extreme dislike

2. ILSFADIUDN = 2. _____
   Despicable; contemptible

3. ETILVYIABN = 3. _____
   Unavoidably

4. EPERXELDP = 4. _____
   Troubled with uncertainty

5. EPRRODUC = 5. _____
   Got by special effort; obtained

6. GYFSOCFLNI = 6. _____
   Mockingly

7. NNUGMSSUAI = 7. _____
   Modest

8. ODATRI = 8. _____
   Skillful and adept under pressure

9. EDPRU = 9. _____
   One who is excessively concerned with being proper

10. TFLAASTI =10. _____
    One who believes all events are predetermined and inevitable

11. MIORMLAT =11. _____
    Never to be forgotten

12. ALPL =12. _____
    To become dull or boring

13. ITNOAEBST =13. _____
    Stubborn

14. UAEGV =14. _____
    Not clearly expressed; inexplicit

15. PRPESVISOE =15. _____
    Difficult to bear; weighing heavily on the spirit

Anne Frank Vocabulary Juggle Letters 2 Answer Key

1. AHETLO = 1. LOATHE
Hate; extreme dislike

2. ILSFADIUDN = 2. DISDAINFUL
Despicable; contemptible

3. ETILVYIABN = 3. INEVITABLY
Unavoidably

4. EPERXELDP = 4. PERPLEXED
Troubled with uncertainty

5. EPRRODUC = 5. PROCURED
Got by special effort; obtained

6. GYFSOCFLNI = 6. SCOFFINGLY
Mockingly

7. NNUGMSSUAI = 7. UNASSUMING
Modest

8. ODATRI = 8. ADROIT
Skillful and adept under pressure

9. EDPRU = 9. PRUDE
One who is excessively concerned with being proper

10. TFLAASTI = 10. FATALIST
One who believes all events are predetermined and inevitable

11. MIORMLAT = 11. IMMORTAL
Never to be forgotten

12. ALPL = 12. PALL
To become dull or boring

13. ITNOAEBST = 13. OBSTINATE
Stubborn

14. UAEGV = 14. VAGUE
Not clearly expressed; inexplicit

15. PRPESVISOE = 15. OPPRESSIVE
Difficult to bear; weighing heavily on the spirit

Anne Frank Juggle Letters 3

1. NBTISOEAT = 1. _____
   Stubborn

2. AOTIRMML = 2. _____
   Never to be forgotten

3. SDINFUILAD = 3. _____
   Despicable; contemptible

4. OAD = 4. _____
   Bustle; fuss; bother

5. IEVLTANIBY = 5. _____
   Unavoidably

6. TOCIIRPFNE = 6. _____
   Adept; expert

7. EQITSCUHTO = 7. _____
   Characteristic of a woman who makes teasing romantic overtures

8. IND = 8. _____
   Jumble of loud noises

9. PINTEINERMT = 9. _____
   Improperly forward or bold

10. NIGET = 10. _____
    Slight addition

11. OAFLO = 11. _____
    Reserved; remote

12. TAROID = 12. _____
    Skillful and adept under pressure

13. EPRDU = 13. _____
    One who is excessively concerned with being proper

14. IMGNMHAS = 14. _____
    Putting on a false appearance

15. SATIFLAT = 15. _____
    One who believes all events are predetermined and inevitable

Copyrighted

Anne Frank Juggle Letters 3 Answer Key

1. NBTISOEAT = 1. OBSTINATE
   Stubborn

2. AOTIRMML = 2. IMMORTAL
   Never to be forgotten

3. SDINFUILAD = 3. DISDAINFUL
   Despicable; contemptible

4. OAD = 4. ADO
   Bustle; fuss; bother

5. IEVLTANIBY = 5. INEVITABLY
   Unavoidably

6. TOCIIRPFNE = 6. PROFICIENT
   Adept; expert

7. EQITSCUHTO = 7. COQUETTISH
   Characteristic of a woman who makes teasing romantic overtures

8. IND = 8. DIN
   Jumble of loud noises

9. PINTEINERMT = 9. IMPERTINENT
   Improperly forward or bold

10. NIGET = 10. TINGE
    Slight addition

11. OAFLO = 11. ALOOF
    Reserved; remote

12. TAROID = 12. ADROIT
    Skillful and adept under pressure

13. EPRDU = 13. PRUDE
    One who is excessively concerned with being proper

14. IMGNMHAS = 14. SHAMMING
    Putting on a false appearance

15. SATIFLAT = 15. FATALIST
    One who believes all events are predetermined and inevitable

Anne Frank Vocabulary Jugle Letters 4

1. TSCLEAHT = 1. _____
   Personal, movable property

2. ODERPCUR = 2. _____
   Got by special effort; obtained

3. ELSO = 3. _____
   Only

4. IEPDUQ = 4. _____
   Provoked; full of resentment

5. NLESADINTEC = 5. _____
   Kept secret to conceal an improper purpose

6. GITEN = 6. _____
   Slight addition

7. UIANFLDDSI = 7. _____
   Despicable; contemptible

8. AFTANIC = 8. _____
   Person with an extreme enthusiasm for something

9. IEILYABNTV = 9. _____
   Unavoidably

10. UPEOSLURFUS =10. _____
    Not needed

11. YSNOEPUMD =11. _____
    A fictitious name used by an author

12. EESPSOVRPI =12. _____
    Difficult to bear; weighing heavily on the spirit

13. ASNSUNUIMG =13. _____
    Modest

14. FOALO =14. _____
    Reserved; remote

15. ENLODCO =15. _____
    To express sympathy

Anne Frank Vocabulary Juggle Letters 4 Answer Key

1. TSCLEAHT = 1. CHATTELS
Personal, movable property

2. ODERPCUR = 2. PROCURED
Got by special effort; obtained

3. ELSO = 3. SOLE
Only

4. IEPDUQ = 4. PIQUED
Provoked; full of resentment

5. NLESADINTEC = 5. CLANDESTINE
Kept secret to conceal an improper purpose

6. GITEN = 6. TINGE
Slight addition

7. UIANFLDDSI = 7. DISDAINFUL
Despicable; contemptible

8. AFTANIC = 8. FANATIC
Person with an extreme enthusiasm for something

9. IEILYABNTV = 9. INEVITABLY
Unavoidably

10. UPEOSLURFUS =10. SUPERFLUOUS
Not needed

11. YSNOEPUMD =11. PSEUDONYM
A fictitious name used by an author

12. EESPSOVRPI =12. OPPRESSIVE
Difficult to bear; weighing heavily on the spirit

13. ASNSUNUIMG =13. UNASSUMING
Modest

14. FOALO =14. ALOOF
Reserved; remote

15. ENLODCO =15. CONDOLE
To express sympathy

ADO	Bustle; fuss; bother
ADROIT	Skillful and adept under pressure
ALOOF	Reserved; remote
ARDENT	Fervent; passionate
BLISS	Extreme happiness
BOISTEROUS	Loud; lacking in restraint or discipline

CAPITULATION	Surrender under specified conditions
CHATTELS	Personal, movable property
CLANDESTINE	Kept secret to conceal an improper purpose
COMPENSATION	Offset; counterbalance; repayment
CONCEITED	Characterized by holding an unusually high opinion of oneself
CONDOLE	To express sympathy

CONGENIAL	Friendly
COQUETTISH	Characteristic of a woman who makes teasing romantic overtures
DIN	Jumble of loud noises
DISDAINFUL	Despicable; contemptible
FANATIC	Person with an extreme enthusiasm for something
FATALIST	One who believes all events are predetermined and inevitable

FATUOUS	Foolish
IMMORTAL	Never to be forgotten
IMPERTINENT	Improperly forward or bold
INCESSANTLY	Continually, without interruption
INEVITABLY	Unavoidably
LIBERATED	Freed

LOATHE	Hate; extreme dislike
MANIFEST	Show plainly; reveal
NUISANCE	Bother
OBSTINATE	Stubborn
OPPRESSIVE	Difficult to bear; weighing heavily on the spirit
PALL	To become dull or boring

PERPLEXED	Troubled with uncertainty
PIQUED	Provoked; full of resentment
PLIED	Assailed
PRIVATIONS	Lack of basic necessities of life
PROCURED	Got by special effort; obtained
PROFICIENT	Adept; expert

PRUDE	One who is excessively concerned with being proper
PSEUDONYM	A fictitious name used by an author
QUEERLY	Oddly
REBUKE	Reprimand; criticize
SARCASM	Cutting remarks
SCOFFINGLY	Mockingly

SHAMMING	Putting on a false appearance
SOLE	Only
SUPERFLUOUS	Not needed
TACT	Ability to act or speak without offending
TINGE	Slight addition
TOLERANT	Inclined to put up with beliefs, practices or traits of others

UNASSUMING	Modest
VAGUE	Not clearly expressed; inexplicit

Anne Frank

SUPERFLUOUS	CONDOLE	OPPRESSIVE	TOLERANT	CONGENIAL
CONCEITED	TINGE	SARCASM	MANIFEST	FATUOUS
UNASSUMING	CLANDESTINE	FREE SPACE	ALOOF	SHAMMING
PRUDE	VAGUE	REBUKE	OBSTINATE	PALL
ADO	PLIED	PROFICIENT	IMPERTINENT	BOISTEROUS

Anne Frank

PROCURED	INEVITABLY	QUEERLY	LOATHE	BLISS
LIBERATED	COQUETTISH	SCOFFINGLY	CHATTELS	PIQUED
TACT	ARDENT	FREE SPACE	NUISANCE	ADROIT
PSEUDONYM	IMMORTAL	FATALIST	SOLE	PRIVATIONS
FANATIC	COMPENSATION	PERPLEXED	CAPITULATION	DISDAINFUL

Anne Frank

BOISTEROUS	CONCEITED	PRIVATIONS	SUPERFLUOUS	PIQUED
ADO	IMPERTINENT	INCESSANTLY	PALL	FATUOUS
FANATIC	IMMORTAL	FREE SPACE	DISDAINFUL	BLISS
PRUDE	PROCURED	PERPLEXED	VAGUE	MANIFEST
NUISANCE	ARDENT	CONGENIAL	PLIED	CLANDESTINE

Anne Frank

TINGE	SARCASM	SHAMMING	CHATTELS	QUEERLY
ALOOF	CONDOLE	ADROIT	LOATHE	LIBERATED
UNASSUMING	PSEUDONYM	FREE SPACE	PROFICIENT	CAPITULATION
INEVITABLY	TOLERANT	COQUETTISH	TACT	OPPRESSIVE
COMPENSATION	OBSTINATE	SOLE	DIN	SCOFFINGLY

Anne Frank

SOLE	CONGENIAL	OPPRESSIVE	IMMORTAL	CLANDESTINE
DISDAINFUL	SHAMMING	BLISS	CHATTELS	SUPERFLUOUS
PRIVATIONS	LOATHE	FREE SPACE	FATALIST	MANIFEST
PSEUDONYM	QUEERLY	DIN	PALL	FATUOUS
INEVITABLY	PLIED	PRUDE	IMPERTINENT	UNASSUMING

Anne Frank

ALOOF	TINGE	ARDENT	PROCURED	PERPLEXED
SARCASM	TOLERANT	OBSTINATE	CAPITULATION	NUISANCE
TACT	CONDOLE	FREE SPACE	BOISTEROUS	CONCEITED
SCOFFINGLY	PIQUED	VAGUE	LIBERATED	ADROIT
REBUKE	COQUETTISH	ADO	COMPENSATION	PROFICIENT

Anne Frank

SHAMMING	REBUKE	CAPITULATION	OBSTINATE	SUPERFLUOUS
BLISS	FATALIST	ADO	OPPRESSIVE	SARCASM
INEVITABLY	LIBERATED	FREE SPACE	PSEUDONYM	DISDAINFUL
BOISTEROUS	SCOFFINGLY	LOATHE	COQUETTISH	PLIED
UNASSUMING	MANIFEST	TINGE	INCESSANTLY	CONGENIAL

Anne Frank

COMPENSATION	PIQUED	CHATTELS	ADROIT	NUISANCE
DIN	PALL	VAGUE	CONDOLE	IMPERTINENT
PERPLEXED	PROCURED	FREE SPACE	SOLE	FANATIC
PRUDE	FATUOUS	IMMORTAL	ALOOF	PROFICIENT
TOLERANT	CLANDESTINE	CONCEITED	TACT	QUEERLY

Anne Frank

INCESSANTLY	CLANDESTINE	TOLERANT	INEVITABLY	UNASSUMING
PROCURED	COMPENSATION	FANATIC	NUISANCE	TINGE
PALL	PROFICIENT	FREE SPACE	CONGENIAL	CONDOLE
DIN	SHAMMING	FATUOUS	ALOOF	FATALIST
MANIFEST	QUEERLY	COQUETTISH	BOISTEROUS	ADROIT

Anne Frank

BLISS	CAPITULATION	SARCASM	DISDAINFUL	PRUDE
LIBERATED	LOATHE	OPPRESSIVE	PSEUDONYM	SCOFFINGLY
CONCEITED	TACT	FREE SPACE	CHATTELS	IMMORTAL
PIQUED	REBUKE	ARDENT	PLIED	SUPERFLUOUS
VAGUE	ADO	IMPERTINENT	PERPLEXED	OBSTINATE

Anne Frank

ADROIT	CLANDESTINE	SUPERFLUOUS	TOLERANT	BOISTEROUS
TINGE	MANIFEST	CONDOLE	PRIVATIONS	INEVITABLY
QUEERLY	IMMORTAL	FREE SPACE	SCOFFINGLY	ADO
CONCEITED	PIQUED	OBSTINATE	SOLE	FANATIC
LIBERATED	REBUKE	IMPERTINENT	PROCURED	PRUDE

Anne Frank

FATUOUS	SHAMMING	BLISS	CONGENIAL	ARDENT
CHATTELS	OPPRESSIVE	COMPENSATION	SARCASM	PROFICIENT
FATALIST	INCESSANTLY	FREE SPACE	PSEUDONYM	DISDAINFUL
PALL	TACT	DIN	NUISANCE	PERPLEXED
ALOOF	PLIED	VAGUE	UNASSUMING	COQUETTISH

Anne Frank

MANIFEST	PALL	PLIED	FATUOUS	CHATTELS
IMPERTINENT	PERPLEXED	PSEUDONYM	CAPITULATION	INEVITABLY
QUEERLY	BLISS	FREE SPACE	IMMORTAL	ARDENT
COQUETTISH	SCOFFINGLY	OPPRESSIVE	VAGUE	SHAMMING
FANATIC	CONDOLE	COMPENSATION	CONGENIAL	TOLERANT

Anne Frank

PRIVATIONS	DIN	ADO	PRUDE	PROFICIENT
TINGE	REBUKE	DISDAINFUL	ALOOF	PROCURED
ADROIT	SARCASM	FREE SPACE	TACT	PIQUED
OBSTINATE	SUPERFLUOUS	UNASSUMING	SOLE	NUISANCE
FATALIST	BOISTEROUS	CLANDESTINE	INCESSANTLY	LOATHE

Anne Frank

LIBERATED	PLIED	ARDENT	PIQUED	SUPERFLUOUS
ALOOF	PRUDE	CONDOLE	CHATTELS	NUISANCE
FANATIC	BOISTEROUS	FREE SPACE	REBUKE	PALL
OPPRESSIVE	TOLERANT	ADO	ADROIT	CLANDESTINE
SHAMMING	LOATHE	OBSTINATE	SCOFFINGLY	CONGENIAL

Anne Frank

PRIVATIONS	DIN	UNASSUMING	FATALIST	PROFICIENT
QUEERLY	TINGE	INEVITABLY	FATUOUS	COQUETTISH
BLISS	MANIFEST	FREE SPACE	INCESSANTLY	CAPITULATION
PROCURED	IMPERTINENT	DISDAINFUL	PERPLEXED	COMPENSATION
TACT	CONCEITED	PSEUDONYM	SOLE	IMMORTAL

Anne Frank

LOATHE	BOISTEROUS	ADO	PROFICIENT	OBSTINATE
DISDAINFUL	FANATIC	CONDOLE	INCESSANTLY	SHAMMING
FATUOUS	COMPENSATION	FREE SPACE	PROCURED	CHATTELS
TOLERANT	PERPLEXED	SUPERFLUOUS	CAPITULATION	BLISS
PLIED	QUEERLY	CLANDESTINE	TACT	SOLE

Anne Frank

PRUDE	ADROIT	NUISANCE	INEVITABLY	CONGENIAL
COQUETTISH	VAGUE	IMPERTINENT	TINGE	SARCASM
DIN	UNASSUMING	FREE SPACE	SCOFFINGLY	PIQUED
OPPRESSIVE	REBUKE	PSEUDONYM	IMMORTAL	FATALIST
ALOOF	PALL	CONCEITED	MANIFEST	ARDENT

Anne Frank

PALL	CONCEITED	FATALIST	PROCURED	TACT
ADROIT	BOISTEROUS	NUISANCE	QUEERLY	ARDENT
ALOOF	CHATTELS	FREE SPACE	PIQUED	INCESSANTLY
REBUKE	OPPRESSIVE	SOLE	FANATIC	PERPLEXED
DISDAINFUL	SUPERFLUOUS	VAGUE	PROFICIENT	PRIVATIONS

Anne Frank

ADO	CAPITULATION	SHAMMING	IMPERTINENT	UNASSUMING
CONDOLE	DIN	SCOFFINGLY	TINGE	INEVITABLY
TOLERANT	FATUOUS	FREE SPACE	LIBERATED	PSEUDONYM
LOATHE	CLANDESTINE	PRUDE	SARCASM	IMMORTAL
COMPENSATION	CONGENIAL	COQUETTISH	MANIFEST	BLISS

Anne Frank

OPPRESSIVE	PROCURED	PRUDE	INCESSANTLY	SHAMMING
UNASSUMING	COMPENSATION	NUISANCE	PALL	IMPERTINENT
PLIED	SOLE	FREE SPACE	BOISTEROUS	PRIVATIONS
ADROIT	ARDENT	ALOOF	TINGE	DIN
OBSTINATE	FATALIST	FANATIC	SCOFFINGLY	ADO

Anne Frank

PROFICIENT	REBUKE	DISDAINFUL	PIQUED	CLANDESTINE
FATUOUS	MANIFEST	CONCEITED	SUPERFLUOUS	TOLERANT
COQUETTISH	PERPLEXED	FREE SPACE	TACT	IMMORTAL
CONDOLE	LIBERATED	INEVITABLY	CHATTELS	PSEUDONYM
CONGENIAL	LOATHE	SARCASM	VAGUE	QUEERLY

Anne Frank

PALL	SUPERFLUOUS	ARDENT	OBSTINATE	VAGUE
PROCURED	REBUKE	NUISANCE	ADROIT	TOLERANT
CAPITULATION	TINGE	FREE SPACE	QUEERLY	BOISTEROUS
TACT	SARCASM	PLIED	UNASSUMING	FATUOUS
CONDOLE	INCESSANTLY	DISDAINFUL	FANATIC	CONGENIAL

Anne Frank

PSEUDONYM	LIBERATED	CLANDESTINE	SCOFFINGLY	COQUETTISH
PERPLEXED	OPPRESSIVE	IMPERTINENT	IMMORTAL	DIN
PIQUED	CONCEITED	FREE SPACE	ALOOF	ADO
FATALIST	INEVITABLY	PRUDE	LOATHE	SOLE
MANIFEST	COMPENSATION	PROFICIENT	SHAMMING	CHATTELS

Anne Frank

SOLE	BLISS	COQUETTISH	CHATTELS	ADO
CONGENIAL	REBUKE	LOATHE	QUEERLY	CLANDESTINE
PRIVATIONS	SCOFFINGLY	FREE SPACE	CONDOLE	CAPITULATION
SARCASM	ADROIT	BOISTEROUS	TACT	SHAMMING
IMMORTAL	PLIED	SUPERFLUOUS	LIBERATED	OPPRESSIVE

Anne Frank

TINGE	COMPENSATION	PROFICIENT	TOLERANT	UNASSUMING
PERPLEXED	OBSTINATE	PRUDE	INCESSANTLY	PSEUDONYM
FANATIC	INEVITABLY	FREE SPACE	ALOOF	CONCEITED
FATALIST	IMPERTINENT	VAGUE	DIN	NUISANCE
PALL	MANIFEST	PROCURED	DISDAINFUL	ARDENT

Anne Frank

NUISANCE	PROFICIENT	VAGUE	ADO	CONCEITED
IMMORTAL	PROCURED	CAPITULATION	FATUOUS	ADROIT
SOLE	PALL	FREE SPACE	TACT	ALOOF
PLIED	REBUKE	ARDENT	DISDAINFUL	COMPENSATION
FATALIST	PERPLEXED	CONGENIAL	TOLERANT	CLANDESTINE

Anne Frank

UNASSUMING	INCESSANTLY	OPPRESSIVE	MANIFEST	BOISTEROUS
IMPERTINENT	PSEUDONYM	COQUETTISH	SARCASM	BLISS
OBSTINATE	QUEERLY	FREE SPACE	TINGE	PRIVATIONS
SHAMMING	LOATHE	SUPERFLUOUS	LIBERATED	CHATTELS
FANATIC	CONDOLE	SCOFFINGLY	INEVITABLY	DIN

Anne Frank

PRUDE	PIQUED	TOLERANT	REBUKE	INCESSANTLY
PRIVATIONS	COMPENSATION	IMMORTAL	OBSTINATE	ALOOF
ADO	SUPERFLUOUS	FREE SPACE	FATUOUS	CLANDESTINE
UNASSUMING	QUEERLY	DISDAINFUL	PROFICIENT	SOLE
CONDOLE	BLISS	LOATHE	PROCURED	LIBERATED

Anne Frank

PERPLEXED	OPPRESSIVE	TINGE	FANATIC	CAPITULATION
MANIFEST	CHATTELS	BOISTEROUS	IMPERTINENT	PALL
CONCEITED	COQUETTISH	FREE SPACE	VAGUE	PSEUDONYM
INEVITABLY	DIN	NUISANCE	SARCASM	CONGENIAL
ADROIT	SHAMMING	TACT	ARDENT	FATALIST

Anne Frank

PALL	SUPERFLUOUS	INEVITABLY	FATALIST	CONGENIAL
PERPLEXED	QUEERLY	SOLE	ADO	COMPENSATION
TINGE	INCESSANTLY	FREE SPACE	PLIED	CAPITULATION
LOATHE	UNASSUMING	BOISTEROUS	DISDAINFUL	PROCURED
CLANDESTINE	PROFICIENT	TOLERANT	CONDOLE	ADROIT

Anne Frank

SHAMMING	NUISANCE	REBUKE	PRUDE	OBSTINATE
OPPRESSIVE	CONCEITED	ALOOF	PRIVATIONS	MANIFEST
ARDENT	COQUETTISH	FREE SPACE	LIBERATED	DIN
PSEUDONYM	FATUOUS	TACT	BLISS	SARCASM
VAGUE	IMMORTAL	CHATTELS	SCOFFINGLY	PIQUED